Good Lives and Moral Education

Studies in Moral Philosophy

John Kekes
General Editor

Vol. 4

PETER LANG
New York • Bern • Frankfurt am Main • Paris

Evan Simpson

Good Lives and Moral Education

PETER LANG

New York • Bern • Frankfurt am Main • Paris

Library of Congress Cataloging-in-Publication Data

Simpson, Evan
　　Good lives and moral education.

　　(Studies in moral philosophy ; vol. 4)
　　Bibliography: p.
　　Includes index.
　　1. Moral education.　2. Ethics.　I. Title.　II. Series.
LC268.S49　　　1989　　　370.11'4　　　88-31509
ISBN 0-8204-1079-9
ISSN 0899-4897

CIP-Titelaufnahme der Deutschen Bibliothek

Simpson, Evan:
Good lives and moral education / Evan Simpson.
— New York; Bern; Frankfurt am Main; Paris:
Lang, 1989.
　　(Studies in Moral Philosophy; Vol. 4)
　　ISBN 0-8204-1079-9

NE: GT

© Peter Lang Publishing, Inc., New York 1989

Printed by Weihert-Druck GmbH, Darmstadt, West Germany

For Miriam

Contents

Preface

Some of the material in this essay initially appeared in the following places. I am grateful to the publishers of the books and journals for permission to use the discussions again here. Full bibliographical details of these works and all those mentioned in notes to the text are given in the bibliography.

Chapter 1 includes fragments of the introduction to Stanley G. Clarke and Evan Simpson, eds., *Anti-Theory in Ethics and Moral Conservatism*, copyright © 1989 by State University of New York Press, as well as parts of my paper, "Moral Conservatism," in *The Review of Politics*.

Chapters 2 and 4 divide my article, "Emile's Moral Development: A Rousseauan Perspective on Kohlberg," from *Human Development*. Chapter 4 also includes much of "A Values-Clarification Retrospective," which appeared in *Educational Theory*.

Chapter 5 includes a portion of "Moral Conservatism" and much of "The Development of Political Reasoning" as published in *Human Development*. The latter article and "Emile's Moral Development" are used with the permission of S. Karger AG, Basel.

Most of the first three chapters and the latter part of chapter 5 are new.

The views stated below have developed over a number of years, during which I have benefited from conversations with my friend and collaborator Stanley G. Clarke, my colleague Louis Greenspan, and my daughter Thel. I thank them all, along with the many other generous people not named here.

Introduction

At its best philosophy is a liberating activity, challenging myths which support the *status quo* and describing conceivable alternatives to existing practices. Questioning assumptions, testing arguments, describing novel possibilities, philosophy is also inherently controversial. Because disagreements are central to the subject, philosophical inquiry does not converge on an ever more accurate picture of the way things really are, in contrast to the ideal of scientific theory. The absence of such a fixed standard will be welcomed rather than regretted unless we suppose that scientific knowledge is more valuable than other kinds – an assumption itself open to challenge as failing to recognize the importance of philosophy in understanding ourselves.

Moral philosophy is crucial to self-understanding and naturally mirrors these disagreements. It may also help to moderate them by convincing us that the search for fixed ethical standards is a mistake. In so doing, however, moral philosophy challenges one of its modern expressions. The objective of modern moral theory has been to define principles governing all rational persons, determining the correct action in situations which require choice, and thus settling disagreements. But moral theory has never approached its ideal, and the universal principles it searches for are problematical. Many have been proposed, but philosophers have not agreed on which to support even when they have agreed in their actual moral judgments and practices. The connection between principle and practice is thus unclear, and the methods of moral philosophy associated with Kant, Bentham, and their successors have lost much of their appeal. Moral philosophy, at least for now, may do better if freed from moral theory.[1]

The most instructive way of exploring questions about ethical judgment at this time is to examine moral particulars – actual practices, customs, and traditions. Motivated by this hope, attention has recently been directed to the special obligations of filial and sexual morality, to the morality of trust and friendship, and to the art of fiction as an expression of moral thinking. These discussions avoid the assumption that moral philosophy is like science, finding nothing in morality which requires the kind of explanation or justification which theories are designed to give.

Recent work by moral educators also helps to make this case. In examining the reasons they advance for their recommendations, we find philosophical theories entwined with psychology and become able to disentangle these theories from practical prescriptions. Then we have reason to ask whether the practices can be defended without these assumptions. We find that some of them cannot be, while others are more defensible without the theories rather than less.

There is a second advantage in this approach and attention to this subject-matter. The writings of educators present issues starkly, much more so than we find in sophisticated philosophical embellishments on conceptions established in the seventeenth and eighteenth centuries. These often brilliant explorations differ from their predecessors mainly in detail. This detail is highly interesting to scholars but not particularly useful in understanding actual moral judgment. For that, a different kind of detail is needed. We need first of all to understand the complexities of belief and motive which characterize the fine-grained personal relationships of interest to novelists, psychiatrists, and casuists.

The appropriateness of seeing moral philosophy through moral education later in this essay is further heightened by relationships between philosophy and knowledge, knowledge and education. "All men by nature desire to know," Aristotle said at the beginning of his *Metaphysics*. "It is owing to their wonder that men both now begin and at first began to philosophize, i.e., to seek wisdom, or knowledge."[2] Moral philosophy seeks moral knowledge, and its limits are the limits of moral education. There is something to learn only if there is something to know, so that educational practices (whether in schools or elsewhere, whether of children or adults) are of natural interest to moral philosophy.

A frequent presence in this discussion is Lawrence Kohlberg. He has produced one of the most interesting and thoughtful attempts at an adequate philosophical theory of moral education. His account and others like it serve as excellent foils for the alternative conception developed here. The central idea of this alternative is the good for human beings – a notion whose diminished stature is reflected in the priority given to principles in moral theory. This good belongs to a view of human development which honors emotion as highly as intellect, giving a central place to wonder and other feelings of interest to moral philosophy.

Against the assumptions of the main schools of moral education a less abstract and theoretical conception of moral philosophy and moral argument emerges. We are reminded that moral education aims less at skill in calculation and inference than at practices of living. We also find that human psychology is more convincing as a basis for these practices than undemonstrable metaphysical notions of "common humanity." It is useful to ask with Hume, "Would you know the sentiments, inclinations, and course of life of the Greeks and Romans? Study well the temper and actions of the French and English...."[3] The constancy in human manners and motivations which survives differences of history and custom is philosophically important, although it has no special philosophical support.

The following treatment of these matters falls into five main parts.

1. What is moral philosophy?

In order to understand the practice of moral philosophy, we need some sense of the range of answers to the question, what is morality? This is itself a controversial matter. The modern tendency to understand morality in terms of universal principles of right action is challenged by a back-to-Aristotle movement stressing the centrality of good and virtue. Major issues are often obscured by a war of words (R.S. Peters describes an opponent as "allergic to principles" while Stephen Toulmin condemns "the tyranny of principles"[4]), but the debate properly centers on the relationship between the abstractions of moral theory and the concrete ethical life. The desirability of kindness, modesty, and many other virtuous traits cannot be accounted for by appeal to principles. Since their exclusion from the sphere of morality would be arbitrary, many ethical requirements are inexplicable from the standpoint of rationalistic moral philosophy.

The inadequacy of rationalistic conceptions of morality motivates setting aside moral theory in favor of close description of moral customs and patterns of emotional response. So seen, the philosophical study of morality requires more sensitivity to the meaning of particular situations than to universally valid patterns of inference between general principles and moral choice. It's not that morality is "unprincipled" but that there are moral conflicts which theoretically sanctioned principles cannot resolve. As a result, it often seems more plausible to regard theories and principles as expressions of particular moral and political values rather than as grounds for these values. This viewpoint rules out critically assessing moral opinion and sentiment from any superior perspective, and in this respect it endorses a conservative appreciation of the virtues prized by particular communities. However it also suggests that immanent or internal criticism of habits of thought and behavior is a central and inevitable form of moral thinking.

Received opinions in moral education represent an entirely opposite doctrine – theorism at its strongest. Within the dominant view statements about kind, modest, courageous, compassionate, honest, or prudent behavior do not qualify as claims which can be critically assessed but as expressions of personal or social approval. They express wishy-washiness rather than morality. The objects of moral knowledge are therefore limited

to rational principles of choice. In order to challenge this orthodoxy effectively and find modern meaning for the idea that
virtue can be taught, we need to explore a view of moral education as related more directly to character than to action. On this
view, the point of moral education is promoting a desirable way
of life rather than following principles of right action as defined
by normative theory.

2. *The good life*

A serious program of moral education reflects a view of human
nature and development. Any positive account of virtue or the
good also needs to take an interest in questions of moral psychology. Alasdair MacIntyre notes that "the virtues, however
conceived, always must stand in some determinate relationship
to the passions, and any cogent account of the virtues requires
at its foundation a cogent account of the passions and their relationship to reason."[5] As an extension of this Aristotelian point,
the concept of well being can not be separated from our emotional, and ultimately biological, makeup. We share a body of
distinctively emotional purposes whose satisfaction is crucial for
happiness. These needs define a family of universal agreements
entirely different in kind from those sought by modern moral
theory.

Rousseau's account of Emile's education illustrates this conception very clearly. *Emile or On Education* is at variance with recent conceptions of morality and moral philosophy in depicting
moral development as including a central role for emotions. The
emotions assert a natural moral law on which we can agree.
The content of this law is largely a matter of social interpretation, however, and this entails the permanent possibility of
moral disagreement in matters of practice. Conflicting conceptions of the good are thus a fact of the moral life. Only the overall structure of conceptions of human well-being remains constant.

The existence of this common structure shows that there is a natural if not a philosophical ground for moral beliefs. At the same time it leaves views of moral truth open to skeptical doubt. If moral judgments are inherently contestable, what justification can there be for regarding some of them as correct? There is an important sense in which William Empson's "This Last Pain" gets it right in saying

> All those large dreams by which men long live well
> Are magic-lanterned on the smoke of hell;
> This then is real, I have implied,
> A painted, small, transparent slide.

Virtues and other elements of the good life are fictive realities, imaginative discoveries. We must "Feign then what's by a decent tact believed," imagine "What could not possibly be there / And learn a style from a despair."[6]

The contestability of moral judgments, the amenability of natural agreements to divergent interpretations, can prompt a darker vision of human dreams: the absence of a single answer to the question of the good life is the disaster of modernity.

> Things fall apart; the centre cannot hold;
> Mere anarchy is loosed upon the world,
> The blood-dimmed tide is loosed ...

Where the poet, W.B. Yeats, foresees the coming of a "dark beast," MacIntyre seeks a "new Saint Benedict,"[7] but prophecy is not work for philosophers. We here ask how the imaginative nature of moral realities can be consistent with the validity of our criteria of moral judgment. Assessing the adequacy of these criteria – including established conventions, accepted canons of criticism, and processes of reaching rational consensus – requires a fuller account of emotional perception, or something like an epistemology for emotional judgments which explains what it means to speak of educating the emotions.

3. *Educating the emotions?*

If human well being is best understood in terms of biologically grounded and culturally specific aspects of emotion, then some tenets of modern psychology obscure options in moral philosophy. A central figure here is John Dewey, whose instrumentalist philosophy establishes room for informed choice but not for rational ends. In this it agrees with a theory of evaluation common in the human sciences. This theory supports an assimilation of practical to technical reasoning, a dichotomy between judging and feeling, and a pedagogical bias towards thinking. It is also extremely influential, being invoked both by contemporary pragmatists who deplore philosophical theory and by moral educators who presuppose it.

Serious attention to emotions adds a necessary dimension to Dewey's psychological views. Because emotions are salient for action, emotional perception is practical perception in which judgment, desire, and feeling are "internally related." Improving our emotional vision through reflection on complex human situations constitutes a form of moral education far removed from the ideal of most modern philosophers. It brings fine awareness and rich responsibility of a kind not possible through abstract deliberation on contextless problem situations. Its natural vehicles are great literature and extended conversation.

Many questions arise during this excursion into epistemology. Treating emotion as a form of perception requires explaining what appear to be crucial disanalogies with sensory awareness, or deep distinctions between the perception of the world as it is in itself and imaginative emotional discoveries. Addressing these problems shows that our evaluative vision can be improved only by tracing moral thinking beyond "nature" and "culture" to communicative practices ranging from solitary reading to public debate. In various ways, Hans-Georg Gadamer, Paulo Freire, and Jürgen Habermas suggest how this can be done and in so doing indicate very clearly the weaknesses of contemporary views of moral education. Together they imply that similarities in the assumptions of Values Clarificationists and cognitive developmentalists are far more interesting than their differences.

4. Education for Choice

The Socratic question, "Can virtue be taught?," is simply rhetorical if one believes there are no virtues. Then moral knowledge is confined to the mastery of abstract principles of choice. If knowledge is the aim of education, it follows that only these principles can be proper objects of moral instruction. On this view, moral education does not tell us how to act, but it enables us to decide how to act. By displaying the shortcomings of this preoccupation with choice we may better appreciate the contrary conception which sees moral education as seeking to build character, improve emotional vision, encourage political reflection, and influence action indirectly in these various ways.

Kohlberg's views include a scheme of moral development remarkably similar to Rousseau's, but he explains stage-development in a very different way, discounting the role of emotions in cognitive change and elaborating theoretical assumptions shared with Values Clarification. Both deny any possibility of a critical sense of the good life by embracing semantical analyses of moral concepts as if they were results of empirical inquiry. Both depend crucially upon a mistaken view of the conventionality of emotional judgment which makes them unduly suspicious of tradition and habit.

The problem of educators like Kohlberg and Values Clarificationists is that they see no possibility of defending and promoting their moral and political instincts except though a philosophical theory which justifies them permanently. The deep problems which afflict these theories force the conclusion that if contemporary practices of moral education are to be considered legitimate they require justification through a more comprehensive and less problematical understanding of human development.

5. Human development

The conception of moral philosophy examined here prompts interesting questions for the notion of human development. Since no external standard is available for assessing progress, no clear distinction can be drawn between moral growth and the unguided evolution of moral viewpoints. The Rousseauan story of human nature and the good does provide a partial criterion by identifying stages of childhood development. There seem, however, to be no stages corresponding to the main political moralities. Here we have only alternative conceptions of right action, no one of which can establish superiority over the others.

Even so, we are not entirely stymied by relativistic puzzlement. The processes of moral argument examined throughout this essay are consistent with communicative practices which have the capacity to test old understandings and generate new ones. An interpretation of some of Habermas's work shows how something like human development can be identified without encountering the problems which beset attempts to enlist developmental psychology into the cause of moral theory. Linking moral, aesthetic, religious, and political education together, it also serves to reconnect aspects of life severed in modern philosophy.

This work is concerned to define avenues for moral philosophy rather than to predict the outcome of future moral argument. The institutions of public discourse sketched here will not develop easily in a world that has only a dim sense of public meanings, and the very idea of such institutions raises a number of difficult questions. Yet they represent possibilities that demand attention. They provide a way of defending something like the set of liberal values which are too readily dismissed as reflecting a decline rather than an extension of common meanings. They display a fit between the passions, social institutions, and conceptions of humanity which has been given too little attention. Finding these ideas expressed in a conception of moral philosophy and moral education may give new vigor to the ancient notion of the good life.

Chapter 1

What is Moral Philosophy?

I *The concept of morality*

What is morality? As for many Socratic questions the Augus-
tinian answer may be best. "If no one asks me, I know; if someone asks me to explain, I don't know." The difficulty has been
posed in a usefully blunt way by Lawrence Kohlberg and his
former colleague, Carol Gilligan. In explaining his inquiries into
moral development Kohlberg says:

> We are not describing how men formulate different conceptions of the
> good, the good life, intrinsic value or purpose. Nor are we discussing
> how men develop certain kinds of character traits and learn to recognize
> these traits in judgments of approbation and disapprobation. Instead, we
> are concentrating on that aspect of morality that is brought to the fore by
> problematic situations or conflicting claims .... In short, we intend the
> term "moral" to be understood in the restricted sense of referring to situa-
> tions which call for judgments involving deontological concepts such as
> right and wrong ...[1]

This intention goes beyond a harmless stipulation. Kohlberg
slides effortlessly from using the term "moral" in a restricted
sense to supposing that this particular use of the word defines
the scope of answerable moral questions:

> The purpose of morality is modest, to resolve the conflicting claims of
> human beings and groups in fairer and better ways. Moral decisions are
> choices between people's conflicting claims, and worthwhile principles
> are ones which resolve these conflicts in ways that are fair, just, impartial
> .... Acting out of principles of fairness is not necessarily causing the great-
> est good. If there is a greatest good that man can agree on, that is fine.

But when men disagree on the greatest good, one either appeals to the gun or settles for a fair decision.[2]

These comments neatly sum up a conception of moral reasoning as determining rights and resolving competing interests. But morality was traditionally understood to concern human relatedness and responsibility for others as well as the rights of separate individuals. Prior to the ascendancy of the modern ideal of independence, people viewed themselves as naturally tied to their fellows. Moral problems concerned conflicting loyalties as much as competing rights. The concept of caring for others was as important as the concept of fairness, and skepticism about the content of the good life could hardly arise. Gilligan expresses such a conception. She describes those who see

> the moral problem as a problem of care and responsibility in relationships rather than as one of rights and rules. [This fact] ties the development of their moral thinking to changes in their understanding of responsibility and relationships, just as the conception of morality as justice ties development to the logic of equality and reciprocity. Thus the logic underlying an ethic of care is a psychological logic of relationships, which contrasts with the formal logic of fairness that informs the justice approach.[3]

This particular disagreement is complicated by being tied to a dispute about the way that men and women conceive of the moral domain, but the feminist issue is not central for us here. Insofar as such differences exist, they can be explained in terms of customs of child rearing and family life.[4] Even sexists like Rousseau agree that they are not innate differences of perception and response. Moreover, Gilligan's plea for a conception of morality including personal responsibilities as well as formal rights is made by others who stress the importance of special obligations. Filial and sexual morality, unlike "worthwhile principles," often call for treating people differently rather than the same, but the differences are not centrally related to gender.[5]

The matter which will concern us is a further complication hidden by the fact that Kohlberg will now "partially accept Gilligan's differentiation of two orientations in moral judgment"[6] and by her also seeking recognition for both of them rather than one alone. Whereas Gilligan views the conceptions of morality as complementary, Kohlberg continues to insist on the primacy of the "justice" orientation.[7] His view is similar to John Rawls's, who, in spite of numerous clarifications to *A Theory of Justice*, continues to rank "the morality of principles" above "the morality of association."

Even this concession seems illusory. Gilligan's view of "the moral problem" cannot be separated from an appreciation of social virtues, but Kohlberg believes that "there are no traits of character corresponding to the virtues and vices."[8] Virtues and vices are but "labels by which people award praise or blame to others."[9] This semantical thesis profoundly diminishes the second level of moral concern. If Charles Taylor is right, it "marginalizes" or "expunges" languages of qualitative contrast that are "central to our moral thinking and ineradicable from it."[10] As Michael Sandel has said of Rawls's theory, Kohlberg's thesis encourages us to see persons as "wholly without character, without moral depth."[11] If there are no qualities of character which have to be recognized as good, then no moral conditions govern individual desires and one is logically free to pursue whatever aims seem appealing.

The philosophical discussion of these questions has become spirited. On the conception of morality as primarily concerned with principles, Sandel continues, "what separates us is in some important sense prior to what connects us – epistemologically prior as well as morally prior." This "deontological vision is flawed ... as an account of our moral experience ..." in denying "those loyalties and convictions whose moral force consists partly in the fact that living by them is inseparable from understanding ourselves as the particular persons we are – as members of this family or community or nation or people, as bearers of this history, as sons and daughters of that revolution, as citizens of this republic...."[12] In similar vein, Stuart Hampshire says: "Conventions; moral perceptions and feelings; institutions and

loyalties; tradition; historical explanations - these are related features, and ineliminable features, of normal thought about the
conduct of life and about the character and value of persons."[13]
Contesting "the standpoint of modern individualism," Alasdair
MacIntyre also insists that "we all approach our own circumstances as bearers of a particular social identity.... I inherit from
the past of my family, my city, my tribe, my nation, a variety of
debts, inheritances, rightful expectations and obligations. These
constitute the given of my life, my moral starting point. This is
in part what gives my life its own moral particularity,"
determining "what is good for me."[14] The social relationship is
primary.

In some respects this is a conservative conception of morality,
honoring the integrity of communities, their customs and institutions, and prevailing values. Concerned with the particular
virtues of particular cultures, it focusses on traits of character
whose sanction has nothing to do with universal principles. It is,
rather, pluralistic and particularistic, recognizing the diversity of
human groups and the debates which surround the practices in
each. Thus Hampshire stresses "the particularity of the particular case" and adds: "men are not only rational and calculative in
forming and pursuing their ideals and in maintaining rules of
conduct, but they are also in the grip of particular and distinguishable memories and of particular and distinguishing local
passions; and the Aristotelian word to emphasize is
'particular'."[15] Local attachments and historical associations
permeate our desires and purposes, and it is reasonable to respect a multitude of moral requirements. Such a particularism is
hardly distinguishable from Roger Scruton's characterization of
conservatism as arising "directly from the sense that one belongs
to some continuing, and pre-existing social order, and that this
fact is all important in determining what to do."[16] Since there
are rival orders and traditions, a defense of pluralism easily follows. Hampshire sees the diversity of customs, values, attitudes,
and human relationships as "a primary, perhaps the primary,
feature of human nature, species-wide...." To understand "the

4

indispensable and related notions of convention and ways of life" leads to the conclusion that the plurality of values is incompatible with any "definite list of essential virtues."[17]

If this is right, moral claims, moral virtues, and principles of conduct unavoidably collide, and "there must always be moral conflicts which cannot, given the nature of morality, be resolved by any constant and generally acknowledged method of reasoning."[18] The thesis of conflict clearly combats Kohlberg's program. In denying the adequacy of rationalistic conceptions of ethics, however, this kind of moral conservatism has not squarely addressed the issues raised by the competition between conceptions. Philosophers have still to consider the spectrum of opinion about the relationship of rational principles to local understandings and practices. Among moral conservatives, some hold that while there are universal principles "superior" to the norms of particular ways of life, morality also includes custom and convention which cannot be justified by these higher principles. Others hold that principles play a justificatory role only within practices and are themselves justified by the considered moral judgments of the participants. Still others accord to principles no more than a heuristic role as summaries of patterns of approved behavior.

The first of these positions is articulated by Hampshire, who describes two levels of morality, the higher one defined by the familiar principles of rationalistic moral philosophy, the other consisting of "the full, complex morality of the family and of sexual relationships and of friendship in any person's actual way of life."[19] He argues that although morality does make rational requirements they are not generally capable of settling issues which are particular to our local attachments and historical associations. Moral principles "plainly under-determine" the fuller, more complex morality of partiality. "[R]ational argument is not available below the level of the general requirements of fairness and of utility."[20]

Michael Oakeshott occupies the other end of the conservative range, although his account has a clear family resemblance to

Hampshire's "two-level" conception of morality. Oakeshott discriminates two "in many respects ... opposite" forms of the moral life. One prizes "the reflective application of a moral criterion." This is the view of the Rationalist, standing for freedom from obligation to any authority except the authority of "reason." To share this form of the moral life is to be the enemy of prejudice, the merely traditional, customary, habitual. The other form, which in Oakeshott's view should always be dominant, is "a habit of affection and behaviour."[21] It consists in conformity to rules which, as Wittgenstein might say, are learned purely practically.[22] The searching intellect will always find principles which seem to underlie social patterns of approval and disapproval, but these principles "are merely abridgments, abstract definitions, of the coherence which approvals and disapprovals themselves exhibit."[23] Hence this approval and disapproval does not spring from principles or from knowledge of them.

This is an interesting difference. Hampshire is close to Oakeshott in saying, "When one values the customs and morality of one's own society or group as distinctive, one is thinking of them as discriminatory. So far there is no requirement to universalize the prescriptions, implicit or explicit, which govern the customs and values, and to think of the prescriptions as applicable to all men, whatever their condition."[24] Beyond this, such requirements may exist in Hampshire's view. There are certain universal traits of moral rationality embodied in deontological and utilitarian theory. In that upper tier are also located the rights to life and liberty which follow from our "common humanity."[25] The latter view contrasts strongly with Oakeshott, Scruton, and others who reject the rationalist form of the moral life altogether and adopt the Burkeian view that we should make moral claims "not on abstract principles 'as the rights of men,' but as the rights of Englishmen."[26] In calling natural rights "fictions,"[27] MacIntyre suggests that Hampshire's qualified form of moral conservatism is indefensible. There is only a single tier in moral thinking, and there is no point to the philosophical effort to explain the existence of natural rights. If there is anything to explain, it is why we persist in believing in this system of rights. "As with other fictions," Bernard Williams notes in a related connection, "it is a real question whether its working could survive a clear understanding of how it works."[28] We will return to this question in due course.

Middle ground is suggested by Rawls's recent interpretations of his theory of justice, in which moral principles have a systematizing role as well as expressing preexisting patterns of approval. Contrary to Sandel, moral thinking is not viewed as having universalistic aspirations, but as involving reflective testing of existing ethical beliefs against others or against new conceptions presented for exploration. The method of reflective equilibrium treats our actual moral intuitions and sentiments as provisionally fixed starting points and is thus tethered to the understandings and agreements of a particular community. These understandings can be tested against moral principles, but the principles themselves are ethnocentric.[29] On this view, there are basic principles and basic rights, but they are understood in terms of the social practices typical of certain political institutions. In this respect one can value not only the customs of one's society or group as distinctive but also its principles and thus think of them as discriminatory. Even here there is no requirement to universalize prescriptions and think of principles as applicable to all human beings. When we do so think of them, Taylor suggests, "What is really going on is that some forms of ethical reasoning are being privileged over others because in our civilization they come less into dispute or look easier to defend."[30]

The primary dispute addressed here is that between the rationalist ethics of universal principles and the customary ethics of local practices. There are locally favored principles of action, but they seem properly described by Oakeshott and are not central to the rationalist conception. There are also universal practices of a sort, but they will turn out to be consistent with the more conservative conception. A secondary issue is thus the need for a more precise delimitation of a conception of morality within the ethics of practices, assuming that this spectrum of views proves to be the more acceptable.

How, though, is the question of acceptability to be answered? Both views can be attractively described. The rationalist defense of principle often includes a view of the self as standing above social affairs and making practical judgments from an abstract and universal point of view. This can be appealing because it treats individuals as autonomous agents with the responsibility of formulating their personal views of the good. In contrast, to emphasize the essential place of customs and institutions in moral thinking is to suppose that human beings accept a prevailing view of the good. Loyalties, conventions, traditions, and historical explanations cannot be eliminated from normal thought about the conduct of life and individual character, so that the common values of a group are the appropriate criteria of critical inquiry within it. The practice-based conception of morality thus adopts an internal perspective on human life, in contrast to philosophical conceptions which proceed in abstraction from familiar ways of life. Contrary to the rationalist view, we never detach ourselves from our moral starting point, so that the primary source of our obligations and expectations is an inheritance from social institutions. This view, too, can be appealing, especially when the morality of principles is deplored for its reflection of life in an impersonal world governed by abstract understandings which do not discriminate amongst individuals or permit sensitivity to particular circumstances. Pleas for an ethics of relationships then express hope that the "principled" or disinterested standpoint might be replaced in a "caring society" by interest in individual persons.

The many questions generated by this competition of perspectives are not easily decided. How do we judge the lives of some communities and traditions as better than others overall (as we do)? How do we defend our own way of life against abominable ones without appealing to some elements of a rationalistic point of view? In thus appealing to a universalistic morality, do we not presuppose one or another dubious theory of human nature? If we avoid this problem by detaching moral principles from doctrines of our common humanity, how can we defend the principles except by saying we find them compelling? Taylor's observation about the reasons for privileging certain forms of moral thinking then applies: we represent parochial conceptions as universal. The conservative conception thus clearly represents a significant challenge not only to one picture of morality but also to the enterprise and aspirations of philosophical theory. We will have to elaborate this complex challenge in various ways in order to discern a more adequately nuanced view which can be thoroughly tested against objections.

Let us begin from the fact that any adequate view of the concept of morality will include an account of approved behavior. In particular, it will describe the place it gives to virtues, or dispositions to promote socially approved actions. It is difficult or impossible to do this in a general way from the rationalist's point of view, since the properties of many virtues are incompatible with those required by rationalism. For rationalists, the desirability of any genuinely virtuous dispositions to behavior will be explained by their relationship to independently valid moral principles. Our moral approval of honesty and justice, for example, should derive from the principle of utility or Kantian universalizability. But this account is not plausible for humility, kindness, gentleness, and many other ostensibly virtuous traits rarely considered to be rational obligations. In Kohlberg's view it does not even work for honesty, so that only justice can be satisfactorily promoted as a rational ideal. For the rationalist, we should consider whatever socially favored traits of action and character cannot be justified in this way as culturally specific and therefore morally irrelevant. They are of interest to anthropology rather than to ethics.

This begs the central question. To suppose that "kind," "generous," and "gentle" are not terms of moral assessment is to express a view of morality which is artificially narrow unless we have reasons to accept rationalist criteria over others. But the rationalist's only reason is the appeal of these criteria themselves. Such terms of appraisal are central in expressions of moral concern. They make the same kind of unavoidable claim on us that "right" and "ought" seem to, and they cannot reasonably be dismissed simply because they fail to fit a preconceived notion of morality. The fact that words for virtues are more prominent in common use than "ought" and "right" is a further indication that the linguistic focus of recent moral philosophy is part of a challenge to moral sensibilities rather than an explication of them.

If gentleness, humility, generosity, and kindness are considered moral qualities, then the rationalist account faces a more serious complaint than narrow and arbitrary classification. These virtues are not only approved without reference to principles but are also foreign to the principled approach. Gentleness can be risky, since others may respond cruelly or manipulatively to one's friendly approach to their difficulties. However part of the friendly response is setting the danger aside, and no principles govern when to maintain this attitude. To be intelligently gentle includes attending to the details of a situation and being sensitive to the other's response so that one can retreat from gentleness in the face of a threat. Being gentle is thus like taking an experimental stance in order to see what it will bring rather than applying principles known in advance.[31] In short, virtue cannot be generally represented as conscientious adherence to principle. The norms typical of many virtues require the use of judgment in order for us to know how to respond appropriately to the particularity of a situation not adequately governed by general rules.[32]

Many virtuous practices are not explicable in terms of principles. Since appealing to a virtue is sufficient to justify an action belonging to such a practice, this form of non-principled moral judgment cannot be accommodated by rationalist requirements. The rationalist conception of morality can provide a complete catalogue of virtues only by ruling certain of them out as irrelevant to rational moral behavior and deliberation. This is arbitrary because gentleness and other traits of character are morally desireable in spite of their independence from principles. They seem not to be praiseworthy only if the bias of rationalism is operating, and why should that prejudice be preferable to any other?

Another feature of non-principled virtues conflicts with the rationalist assumption. These virtues are essentially imprecise and unrankable norms and their plurality means possibilities of conflict which has no rational resolution. As Hampshire reminds us, the norms which govern family and vocation are more specific than justice or utility might require, and they permit problems to arise which resist resolution by universal principle. Attending to responsibilities towards one's family may conflict with a perceived obligation to fulfil one's notable artistic talents, for example. It is not obvious that justice and utility can find satisfactory purchase here, and they may in other cases be dislodged by local norms. It is far from clear, for example, that there is a correct resolution to every conflict between loyalty to a friend and the obligations of justice. To exclude such norms by fiat is to prescribe a point of view rather than to establish its credentials.

The rationalist might respond to such conflicts by distinguishing the requirements of convention from those of morality. Because customs are not shaped by reason, we should not expect agreement among them and between them and rational principles of justice and utility. This is again an arbitrary move. Many norms which are understood by their adherents to be "moral" have no significant basis in abstract moral principles. Sexual norms involve moral sanctions even though we recognize that their significance has more to do with discarded religious doctrines than with justice or utility. They remain important ways of organizing behavior and are firmly attached to attitudes of respect and guilt which it would be strange to say are not moral ones.

What is left but verbal expedient in dealing with the cluster of issues surrounding the Kohlberg-Gilligan exchange? Pursuing a suggestion from Hegel's discussion of morality and the ethical life, we might distinguish moral questions from ethical ones. That would permit saying that morality consists of the requirements of abstract universal principles while the demands of custom and personal relationships, along with those of love and pity, belong to ethics. Likewise, morality is concerned with questions about right and wrong action, ethics with good and bad – and the good life in particular. Virtues, on such an account, are of ethical rather than moral interest. Again, morality governs relationships between relative strangers and ethics concerns intimate connections, morality being a political notion while ethics has to do with everyday life.

This is not yet very enlightening. An attempt to distinguish between morality and ethics only creates a multitude of new questions about their relationship. If the virtues belong to ethics, what distinguishes ethics from anthropology in a way that makes the demands of virtue valid? If politics creates ethical dilemmas and if wrong actions impair the good life, what becomes of the distinction? When the requirements of morality and ethics conflict, which demand has priority? Hegel thought that moral principles gain concrete content from the customs and traditions of a specific community, but is this necessarily so? Might it be argued forcefully that the distinction does not represent different forms of thought and behavior but that morality as rationalists understand it is simply a particular conception of the ethical life – *Sittlichkeit* dressed up with baseless universalistic pretensions?

These are not questions which can be addressed seriously by arguments about the meaning of words or instincts about their use, and there is no reason to think that all of them have general answers. The distinctions which arouse them do nonetheless have a certain rationale. The political forms of practical reasoning express modes of social connection which depend upon formal rules governing independent lives, impartial or systematic criteria of adjudication defined by laws or rights, in contrast to the vaguer criteria of judgment operating where there are emotional relationships and a common conception of the good. Seen in this way, moralities of rules and moralities of relationships express consciousness of different forms of association. So viewed, rationalistic aspirations are appropriately understood as expressions of practical arrangements rather than as reflections of independently valid principles. In order to test this possibility, we must consider in more explicit detail what it is to study morality philosophically.

II *The philosophical study of morality*

The more we emphasize local custom and practice, the further we move from a conception of philosophy as arbiter of reasons in general, as the determiner of basic reasons for beliefs and actions, or as a guarantor of rationality in a timeless sense. To give up these aspirations, though, raises the difficult questions posed above about assessing, criticizing, and improving our habits of conduct and understanding. Answering these questions as they arise in the context of moral philosophy is an unavoidable obligation for rivals to the rationalistic conception of morality.

Mainstream moral philosophy since the eighteenth century has agreed that its mission is to find a theory providing universal principles which apply systematically to particular cases. Such a theory would systematize and extend our moral judgments so as to provide an unambiguous guide for behavior. These judgments, as characterized by critics like Hampshire and Williams, are thought of as consequences of applying abstract principles to moral problems in an almost computational way, giving a procedure for deducing the morally correct answer in any given circumstances.

Two different conceptions of normative theory lurk in this characterization. The stronger is the rationalistic formulation variously expressed by Richard Brandt's utilitarianism, David Gauthier's contract theory, Thomas Nagel's "view from nowhere," and many other contemporary philosophers. It pursues the ideal of a set of normative principles governing all rational beings and providing a dependable procedure for reaching definite moral judgments and decisions in all cases. This understanding of theory is exemplified by various deontological accounts, which view right action as determined by a system of rules that any rational person would accept, and utilitarian accounts, which regard moral assessments as measures of the capacity of actions or institutions to promote the single rationally acceptable value – individual welfare. The status of principles in this form of theory is foundational in that they justify moral judgments but are not themselves justified by such judgments. Principles are also foundational in that in subsuming practical questions under theoretical ones they entail the fundamental eliminability of casuistic reasonings.

The other conception of moral theory aims for less. It seeks some order in the chaos of phenomena by stressing the systematizing role of moral reflection. The approach is well represented by Rawls's method of reflective equilibrium and by Martha Nussbaum's construal of Aristotelian moral philosophy as proceeding "by way of reflective dialogue between the intuitions and beliefs of the interlocutor, or reader, and a series of complex ethical conceptions, presented for exploration."[33] On this account, a moral theory is the result of already morally educated people finding a harmonious adjustment or readjustment of their considered moral judgments, moral principles, and associated beliefs. On this broadly coherentist conception, normative theories do not necessarily bind all rational beings, and they need not require a unique set of normative principles providing a decision procedure. Here principles are not basic. They do have a justifying role with respect to considered judgments, but the latter also function to justify the principles. "Theory" in this weaker sense is "reasoned reflection." It supports a comprehensive conception of practical judgment which has formal principles and substantive norms as complementary aspects.[34] Since such a theory is connected with the broader conception of "morality" discussed above, it is not the immediate object of our attention. How well it can capture actual and possible practices of reflective moral thinking is a question to be considered later.

Doubts about moral theory complement the belief that local moral practices are primary in practical reasoning. If customary norms provide the basis for the moral interpretation of actions and motives, then it is misguided to seek a ground for social practices in universally applicable normative principles. This anti-theoretical thesis is powerfully stated by Richard Rorty in referring approvingly to "those (like Michael Oakeshott and John Dewey) who want to preserve the institutions [of the liberal democracies] while abandoning their traditional Kantian backup." Annette Baier likewise claims that "there is no room for moral theory as something which is more philosophical and less committed than moral deliberation, and which is not simply an account of our customs and styles of justification, criticism, protest, revolt, conversion, and resolution."[35]

One way of understanding the theoretical project is as a response to the modern decay of historical tradition which, as Baier suggests, left it "hard to see how there could be any such thing as moral philosophy if there were no such thing as 'the moral law.'"[36] So understood the project becomes difficult to take seriously for long. The quest for normative theory is then explained in a way which shows that the theoretical enterprise is the intellectual reflection of a particular historical period rather than an expression of permanent requirements of reason. However in examining moral theory it is not necessary to depend upon this sort of historicist refutation. The difficulties internal to the project are themselves great enough to set it aside.

The slippage between principle and virtue which marks the rationalist conception of morality shows up again in a gap between principle and moral practices in general. If principles are to function as premises in deductive argument, they must have a definite meaning, otherwise they would not entail particular moral judgments. By contrast, the norms of actual moral practices are inherently indefinite. Norms are social standards whose verbal formulation – in the simplest cases, "Don't kill,"

"Don't steal," "Keep promises," – has to be interpreted through a network of cultural understandings if they are not to be purely abstract requirements which do not yet direct action. Their determinate interpretation is provided by the rules of background institutions and ways of life which cannot be precisely spelled out, but this conventional background is essential for the practical understanding of moral imperatives. In short, the properties of principles within rationalist moral theory do not connect with those of norms as they function in moral practices. No path from moral theory to moral practice can be identified, and universal principles cannot fulfill their assigned function.

An appropriate theoretical reply is that imprecise norms guide us well enough in ordinary cases. We agree about their interpretation without having to reconstruct the answer to a practical question as the consequence of a formal inference. It is usually more convenient and efficient to depend upon these customary understandings than to assemble the rational argument leading to the correct practical conclusion. This answer reinforces the assumption that moral theory is capable, in principle and in hard cases, of generating correct answers independently of any appeal to customary norms. To make this rationalistic assumption, though, is only to take for granted that it is possible to close the semantic distance between abstract principles and concrete actions – between, for example, Kant's categorical imperative and telling the truth in dangerous circumstances. It does not close it or indicate how it could be closed.

One might acknowledge this semantic distance but argue that rational principles should not have to justify particular moral judgments directly. It is enough for them to justify the norms of moral practices, thereby justifying the practical judgments conforming to these norms indirectly. This is a precarious line of argument. Justifying a norm requires justifying the background institutions and cultural expectations which determine its content. To justify a prohibition against lying requires defining what lying is. This is a matter of cultural understandings whose justification would require appeal to further principles. These further principles would themselves depend upon justifying still other background interpretations, requiring yet another set of principles, and so on. The distance between norms and the principles meant to justify them cannot be eliminated. Thus, a rationalist formulation of moral principles cannot fully justify the norms of moral practices.

The prior-to-society perspective required for the principles of rationalist moral theory makes them unable to justify the moral practices arising from social history and agreement. Since normative theory is thus faced with deep problems, the practices are left without a sanction, and it becomes unclear what such a sanction might be like. An external justification for our practices may then seem unnecessary, since the very wish for such a justification becomes difficult to understand except as the desire to avoid the painful conflicts and dilemmas generated by moral practices.

Once we cease to think of morality in terms of calculation and deduction from principles, there is no reason to expect a system of moral judgments to be consistent. Conflicts arise because various practices and virtues lead to mutually incompatible obligations, and in the absence of moral theory there is no reason to expect reconcilability of these oppositions to be inherent in moral thinking. It is only because the oppositions are distressing that there is appeal in the rationalist's claim that moral dilemmas, problems, and conflicts, are always resolvable in principle.

Even if we supposed with Hampshire that some moral principles, such as the requirements of justice and benevolence, could be philosophically grounded in universal features of human nature, we would have to follow him in acknowledging that there are also norms which derive from historically specific ways of understanding human needs and capacities. These norms are conventional embellishments of natural humanity. We are carriers of genes, but we order our sexuality through customs of family and kinship which have no ideal rational arrangement. Together with other conventional arrangements they are always liable to make incompatible demands, and while it is often difficult to know whether a moral conflict is resolvable or not, descriptions of the conventional side of morality give reason to believe that some will not be. There is thus a clear and simple "reason for rejecting any rational morality, and moral theory, which could be described as 'abstract and computational'.... [I]t is of the essence of moral problems that on occasion they seem hopeless, incapable of solution, leaving no right action open; this has been an objection not only to utilitarianism of any form, but to any exactly prescribed moral ideal."[37]

In their insistence on the importance of conventional interpretation in moral thinking, anti-theoretical claims describe a hermeneutical turn in moral philosophy. Once this hermeneutical sensitivity arises, it becomes clear that there is no logic of interpretation which embodies a general procedure for deciding moral questions. The interpretations to which most moral concepts are subject create conflicts which cannot be rationally resolved. Concepts for virtues, for example, appear to include elements of both description and evaluation, and they are as a result subject to debate, or "essentially contestable."[38] This explains why, as MacIntyre says, "traditions, when vital, embody continuities of conflict."[39] Every form of human endeavor has its intrinsic goods, and these goods are intrinsically subject to competing interpretations. Every consensus is ambiguous in that it is open to divergent interpretations. No agreement can be considered permanent, and the conflicts which may arise lack necessary or final answers. The knowledge which would be needed to resolve them finally is inherently unobtainable. The contrary view "ignores the place in our cultural history of deep conflicts over what human flourishing and well-being do consist in and the way in which rival and incompatible beliefs on that topic beget rival and incompatible tables of the virtues."[40]

Rejecting rationalistic moral theory does not mean endorsing irrationalism. Instead it may express the possibility of understanding moral reasoning as something else than making logical inferences from principles. It is not to doubt the underlying rationale for seeking principles – the desire to have good reasons for what one does – but to believe that good judgment is required in order to identify these reasons. In this respect the anti-theoretical viewpoint differs markedly from that of a moral skeptic who also rejects rationalism but understands morality in the same way as theorists. Any such negative theorist would see the task of moral philosophy as providing a general test for ethical beliefs and maintain that there can be no such test. The alternative conception of moral philosophy rejects both normative theory and forms of skepticism which assume that morality could only be rational by being suitably connected with a system of universal principles.

In forms like Oakeshott's, the rejection of theoretical conceptions of moral philosophy may extend to denying that the intellectual virtues of theorizing – universality, explicitness, consistency, completeness – are essential to the moral life. In place of these virtues it sees moral rationality as a kind of critical reflection which seeks no support from first principles of any kind. Anti-theorists who question moral theory even in the reflective-equilibrium sense may nevertheless refer to reflective practices in order to advance a positive account of moral rationality. For Baier, these practices constitute dialectical processes of turning natural responses, sentiments and self-interest upon themselves, resulting in adjustments and corrections. For Williams, they aim at using everything available to critical reflection for purposes of making our ethical lives transparent and free of self-deceptions. Although these accounts display commitment to certain values, they ascribe no inherent logic to reflective practices and therefore promote no form of normative theory. Even if these anti-theorists accept the requirement of coherence, they understand it also as requiring interpretation and do not regard it as an independently warrantable demand of reason.

This suggests "relativism," but the anti-theoretical view is no more relativistic than skeptical. In order to see why, consider how people whose conceptions of the good are shaped by different local traditions are to understand and communicate with one another. If there are no foundational principles, no ahistori-

cally valid standards of behavior, then we seem compelled to regard each historical period as a separate world of belief.
"Normal discourse," in which the rules of inquiry and justification are agreed upon, occurs within such worlds, but discussions
with participants in unfamiliar or alien ways of life may lead to
intractable disagreement. But the anti-theoretical view of moral
philosophy does not include these claims, and even if it did it
would not be a form of relativism. Relativism holds that different ethical standards are correct for different groups of people,
so that the same standards may be correct for one group and not
for another. This formula is empty because there are no available criteria of sameness and difference. If substantive accounts
of moral goods and requirements are local accounts, then there
is no identification of goods and requirements across the boundaries of particular ways of life, and no external perspective exists
from which differences can be objectively determined. The alternative to agreement is not separate truths but incomprehen-
sion. Were another society to appear to contradict propositions
we regard as morally certain, we would regard it as deranged.[41]

It is the absence of an external perspective which justifies a
further point of nomenclature. There is no accepted expression
for the positive views of anti-theorists, but it seems accurate to
continue calling them "conservative." They might instead be
summed up as "moral contextualism," "moral conventionalism,"
or "moral pragmatism," but these expressions are either unfamiliar outside academic philosophy or associated with contro-
versies peripheral to this essay.[42] The views of anti-theorists
might also be described in the fashionable language of
"communitarian" accounts which stress custom and tradition
over universal principle. This would be a reasonable alternative
except for disguising the deep conservatism of communitarian
views which accept the common values of a group as the appropriate criteria of critical inquiry within it. Norms of evaluation
on such a view cannot be subjected to critical standards capable
of challenging the fundamental values and practices of the
community.[43] This is conservatism according to almost any-

one's criteria, although it has no particular connection with the political dogma supporting economic privilege, private property, and private schools. It is consistent with the claim of the English socialist R.H. Tawney that "all decent people are at heart conservatives,"[44] and it does not conflict at all with liberal practices and politics where they are well established.[45] It does not even preclude reflective moral agents rejecting some institutional norms, refashioning others, and forging new ones. Edmund Burke recognized that "a state without the means of some change is without the means of its conservation" and that a "principle of conservation" should not exclude a "principle of improvement."[46] Gadamer, too, denies that "the emphasis on tradition which enters all understanding implies an uncritical acceptance of tradition and sociopolitical conservatism.... In truth the confrontation of our historic tradition is always a critical challenge to this tradition."[47] "Conservatism" as it is used here simply opposes the universalistic aspirations of philosophical theories which claim to identify moral standards from a prior-to-society perspective.

If there is a serious problem with the alternative to moral theory, it is not skepticism, relativism, or conservatism. It is that the positive views of anti-theorists remain ill-defined. No clear account has yet been offered of "good reasons," "good judgment," "hermeneutic sensitivity, "reflective practices," or "critical reflection." The most that has been shown is that the pains of disagreement and misunderstanding between and within groups are not necessarily to be regretted. As Rorty has put the point, disagreement includes the possibility of continuing a conversation, whereas the idea that there is a set of final truths to be discovered in moral matters accepts "the freezing-over of culture" and "the dehumanization of human beings."[48]

In the absence of any firm logic of reflection, no well-defined account may be possible. It seems to be Rorty's view that seeking such an account is an expression of "the motives which once led us to posit gods."[49] By rejecting dehumanization we properly "abandon the hope of being anything more than merely human."[50] However in doing so we also open up another possibility. If it is possible to be "merely human," then it may after all be arguable that there are certain points which define our common humanity – not just within a tradition but every-where. As the developmental story related in the following chapter shows, this conception of humanity promises to provide a key of interpretation by which the above problems of interpre-tation can be addressed.

This conception and its requirements will be different in char-acter from anything familiar in moral theory. A fortiori they will also be contrary to the orthodoxies of moral education expressed by the proponents of Values Clarification and by cognitive-de-velopmental psychologists like Kohlberg. An outline of these oppositions gives further definition to the anti-theoretical con-ception of moral philosophy under consideration here.

III *Principle and tradition in moral education*

The official doctrines of mainstream moral education will be elaborated in Chapter 4, but the basic propositions are drawn di-rectly from rationalistic moral theory. The pioneers of Values Clarification insist that values define "an area that isn't a matter of proof or consensus."[51] Kohlberg assumes "that moral judg-ments are not true or false in the cognitive-descriptivist sense,"[52] and that virtues and vices are therefore not describable traits of personality but "labels by which people award praise or blame to others."[53]

Such claims invite the complaint that they depict persons as wholly without character or moral depth because the traits which define character are the virtues and vices, and if there are no such traits there can be no such thing as character.[54] But perhaps, as Kohlberg says, "the fact that there are no traits of character corresponding to the virtues and vices of conventional language should comfort us."[55] It enables us to avoid the wishy-washy habit of letting our moral aims be guided by a desire for approval.[56] We then have reason to welcome moral instruction which does not endorse particular attitudes and actions but only the formal methods of reasoning which can lead to children fashioning their own moral values. If so, we justifiably believe that "the goal of moral education is the stimulation of the 'natural' development of the individual child's own moral judgment and capacities," and we properly demand of any educational practice that it "not entail the violation of the child's moral freedom."[57] We respect "the liberty and rights of the child" only by ensuring that moral principles are self-chosen or self-constructed.[58] This is done by wrestling with moral dilemmas – seeking principles to resolve conflicting interests which are owed respect for their own sake rather than for any claim to validity or worthwhileness.

The trouble is that this conception of morality and moral education expresses philosophical theories which are far from obvious and comforting to many. It contrasts strongly with Oakeshott's view of the moral life as "a habit of affection and conduct" acquired "by living with people who habitually behave in a certain manner."[59] It offends other conservatives, like C.S. Lewis, who reminds readers of his "Reflections on Education" that "until quite modern times all teachers and even all men believed the universe to be such that ... objects did not merely receive, but could merit, our approval or disapproval, our reverence or contempt," and he warns against abandoning "this doctrine of objective value, the belief that certain attitudes are really true, and others really false, to the kind of thing the world is and the kind of things we are."[60]

When sets of assumptions collide, neither view can claim justifiability without producing convincing arguments. Since prevailing orthodoxies implicitly claim validity, however, the conservative challenge has the advantage of being able to throw the burden of proof onto them and to demand that they be defended. If moral educators are to promote the freedom and rights of individuals as properties to be protected and enhanced, it will no longer suffice to appeal to once accepted intuitions. In addition to this rhetorical advantage, moreover, the challengers have a substantial case to make. The only adequate reply to conservative attack may itself be a conservative one. If so, liberal moral education will rest more securely upon tradition than upon philosophical theories of knowledge and morality.

The suggestion is this: in order to retain a sound appreciation of the social value of liberty we should distinguish between liberalism as a set of practices or as a way of life and liberalism as a normative theory. "Liberalism" is a good summary of the legitimate expectations about social relationships which prevail in modern democracies, but the word claims too much when used to suggest that these expectations can be justified by a theory of justice or human nature. So, too, though, for the position of conservatives, like Lewis, who engage in moral theory when basing their case on a realist account of values which makes moral philosophy dependent upon the existence of a moral law ("the Way," "the doctrine of objective value," "Natural Law or Traditional Morality or the First Principles of Practical Reason").[61] In spite of their disagreements, these philosophers and educators are alike in seeking a theoretical backup for the practices they recommend. Conservatives like Oakeshott, however, make little use of philosophical theories, preferring to describe possible forms of life rather than seeking metaphysical and epistemological foundations for them. It is this modest conservatism, with the priority it places on established practices over abstract demonstration which is in issue here.

On such a view, individual rights and freedoms may be regarded as vital goods, but they cannot be derived from general propositions about human nature. Freedoms exist only where there are customs, and the value of rights is owing to that of the other goods which they protect.[62] The primary rights are those which give moral and legal protection to the goods which are essential conditions of individual well-being within a way of life. Since these goods are tied to social practices, the corresponding rights are expressions of a culture's history, tradition, and the expectations they generate. In our society the goods in question include such liberal values as political and religious freedom, together with protections that are often understood by liberals to follow from natural rights to equality and independence. By understanding all goods as social goods rather than as things made good by human nature, however, conservatives deny any basic difference between the rights enjoyed by citizens of liberal democracies and the traditional rights which exist in any human community. Our rights owe their importance to certain central customs whose significance for us carries no implications of permanent authority, Nature having no preference for liberal constitutional regimes over others.

This thesis is present in Rawls's characterization of liberty as a set of particular liberties. The claim that "each person is to have an equal right to the most extensive basic liberty compatible with a similar liberty for others" refers not to an abstract condition but to the items on a list. The basic liberties are: political liberty, together with freedom of speech and assembly; freedom of the person along with the right to hold personal property; freedom from arbitrary arrest and seizure; liberty of conscience and freedom of thought.[63] All of these liberties are understood in terms of the social practices typical of our political institutions.

Political liberty, Rawls explains, is the right to vote and to be eligible for public office. This freedom is evidently inseparable from electoral practices, although (as noted below) there are other conceivable modes of democratic choice and administration. Freedom of speech and assembly likewise exist in a meaningful sense only in a competitive scheme which includes a plurality of associations and interest-groups.[64] As has been clear since Rousseau and Hume, the right to hold property is best specified in terms of practices which differentiate ownership from possession and create privileged claims to certain goods. So, too, for the protection from arrest and seizure, whose existence presupposes institutions of government which have replaced the private enforcement of one's interests within a "state of nature." This right is a protection against the state and would not have to be claimed were anarchistic ideals ever realized. Here too the ascription of rights goes together with political arrangements rather than features of human nature. If this is so, then none of these rights defines an unrevisable moral constraint, since acceptable forms of social organization which do not include them can at least be imagined.

The appeal to imaginary social worlds is only meant to accentuate the relationship between specific rights and particular political regimes. It leaves open the possibility that certain generic rights exist in any political society. All of Rawls's liberties (though not his principle for distributing them) are supported in Burke's writings; only their meaning for practical purposes is different. The specific content of rights – what counts as property, for example – depends upon their interpretation within particular institutions. Thus, Rawls is careful not to state permissions which the right to personal property must include, explicitly recognizing the possible justice of a society in which there is no personal right to capital. Such a state of affairs need not constitute a restraint upon liberty as he carefully defines it. The point can be taken further. The absence of familiar political rights would not necessarily restrain freedom. Restraints do exist where political liberty in Rawls's sense is unequal, since some persons then have fewer votes than others, or some persons' votes are weighted less heavily, or some do not enjoy the benefits of the franchise. It is not voting, however, but consultation, argument, discussion, and debate aiming at broad consensus which are at the heart of democratic regimes. As Bernard Crick observes, "all industrial and industrializing states are democracies ... they all depend on the consent of the majority, as peasant cultures never did."[65] Popular government needs good institutions of communication, but these institutions do not have to include political liberty in Rawls's narrow sense. To resort again to imagination, it is possible that communicative practices should be so pervasive and powerful that the popular will could be asserted through argument leading to agreement rather than being indirectly and imperfectly expressed through periodic elections. Under such circumstances the absence of the right to vote is not an offence against the generic idea of political liberty which Rawls and Burke alike accept.

In addition to the generic rights which can be identified in any political society, all parties can acknowledge an abstract sense in which we may demand the protection of freedom rather than of the specific freedoms which are part of our particular traditions. Human agents need freedom in that agency consists in power to act. It is a mistake, however, to conflate this truism with a meta-physics of human nature which is supposed to ground certain specific protections. This happens when moral theorists speak of "personal projects as the foundation for basic rights" or claim a right possessed "simply as human beings with the capacity to make plans and give justice."[66] Projects and plans of some kind are open to people in every culture. They correspond to what-ever rights are customary in one's society, that is, to the possi-bilities for action created by the rules of existing institutions and by informal expectations which define the normal latitudes of individuality. The conventionality of these practices and expec-tations makes it clear both that we do have rights and that no metaphysical argument shows that we should have them.[67] The conventions exist, and the rights they include therefore do so as well; but conventions are founded not on philosophical theory but on social history and agreement.

It is not uncommon to find such ideas elaborated by political conservatives who believe that rights can exist only where social compulsion does as well. They are also expected from radical critics of the liberal tradition who view political society as occu-pying a middle period of human development. But it is most in-teresting to find them arising among anti-theoretical conserva-tives who happen to be political liberals or social democrats, as when Hampshire insists that abstract principles of justice cannot determine the complex morality of such central social institu-tions as friendship, the family, and sexual relationships. There will always be a sexual morality, but "it does not have to be the same sexual morality with the same restraints and prescription." No rational requirements determine the proper behavior of single persons, polygamists, homosexuals, priests, etc., because freedoms and prohibitions are determined by custom. Michael Walzer likewise bases a recent argument for an egalitarian conception of justice upon rights that "follow from shared conceptions of social goods; they are local and particular in character."[68]

This account of Rawls's concept of freedom makes it possible to treat Walzer and Hampshire as developing implicit features of his view. They describe the direction of Rawls's explicit thinking since the appearance of *A Theory of Justice*. There he was widely understood to subscribe to the notion that political principles require a philosophical grounding, but he has now clearly detached the universalist goals of moral theory from the method of reflective equilibrium and its treatment of existing moral intuitions and sentiments as provisionally fixed starting points. By clearing up this ambiguity he has accepted the anti-theoretical viewpoint that defensible principles of justice are ethnocentric.[69] By dropping the rationalist claim to ahistorical support, the account comes to rest on the understandings and agreements of a particular community, as moral conservatives insist must be the case.

This liberal/conservative agreement is not always easily sustained. Illiberal institutions intrude rudely upon the conservative picture, as when Walzer says of Indian caste society that justice "cannot require a radical redesign of the village against the shared understandings of the members."[70] While such tolerance for gross social distinctions may offend intuitions prevalent in our local culture, justice would be tyrannical if it required a revolution against the self-conceptions of the community. There is no philosophical remedy for this intuitive uneasiness if the liberal case is only the expression of a particular, social conception of the good. It is all very well to claim a special moral status for freedom, but if significant freedoms are themselves customary, liberal traditions can display no inherent advantage over authoritarian ones. To defend freedom is then to defend a particular way of life, but one whose evident superiority lies only in the fact that those whose life it is owe their identities to it.

Now, there is a standard way of arguing that liberal institutions are advanced over others without making a question-begging appeal to freedom as the criterion of development. Caste societies are sustained by conceptions of humanity and the cosmos which have no reasonable claim to truth. Self-conceptions in all traditional societies are colored by systematic forms of false consciousness which do not contaminate perceptions in a culture which has acquired habits of critical reflection. Since the avoidance of error and illusion is desirable, this epistemic criterion provides the impartial standard required for favoring liberal institutions.

It is all too easy for radicals to dismiss this virtue as itself a disguised expression of the ideological fiction of autonomous selves. Political conservatives may also reject it on the grounds that pleasing illusions are an essential part of human well being. Anti-theoretical conservatives do neither, regarding the accounts of society and human nature which sustain such critiques as unenlightening. As Baier says, "Unmasking is a game that has become boring due to the laxness of its rules."[71]

The need to stress active capacities over "impartial standards" can be explained by the peculiar difficulty of resorting to philosophical theories in order to justify a preference for liberal principles. Viewing traditional cosmologies and conceptions of human nature as ridden with error makes them unable to gain or retain one's allegiance. The skepticism about the good which is so common amongst educators should have the same effect upon the commitments which conservatives view as part of the legitimate province of moral education. But these are the commitments which freedoms of thought and conscience are meant to protect, and the freedoms become meaningless if those commitments are undermined by a theory which denies that they are objects of knowledge.

In order for the issue to be clear, we need to remember that skepticism about the good is consistent with acceptance of a kind of moral knowledge common to many liberal theorists, namely knowledge of rational principles of justice and utility and the natural rights they govern. The problem with these impartial standards, we have seen, is their inadequacy for resolving many matters which are subjects of dispute. They do not address the special obligations of sexual or filial morality or give a rationale for the virtues. These things occupy the area of character, subjectivity, and convention which liberal theory deems to fall outside morality or moral knowledge. This is the area of personal conceptions of the good, where, lacking the defense of truth, we appear to need the protection of rights.

The protection we want from doctrines which could suppress the ability to hold and act on our own convictions is provided by the right to liberty of conscience – the right to hold and cherish those optional private beliefs which are central to personal identity and without which nothing else is meaningful. Within the liberal way of life, therefore, no particular vision of the good can be binding upon people generally. Rawls's picturesque statement of this point is that we can perceive no such goods behind the veil of ignorance where we station ourselves for the purpose of deliberating about justice: there is only the thinnest conception of the good on which people can agree. We may feel supremely certain that our commitments are worthy, but we also know that other persons may have contrary views of which they are equally certain – and that sometimes there is no way of defeating those opinions except through the use of force without right.

We suppose, then, that there is no relevant knowledge in the area of personal commitments which concerns us. The problem is that it now becomes difficult to explain the hold of these obligations upon us. When they bind us, it is because we are certain in our convictions, but where there is no knowledge there should be no such confidence. Why then should we be interested in a right to freedom of conscience? That is a protection for beliefs important to people, but they lose their importance when their claim to truth is recognized as illusory. Of course we still want protection against fanatics who would persecute non-believers _ but this protection does not have to be claimed on the grounds of freedom of conscience. That freedom is not a good if we have no conscientious beliefs which we want to defend. The protection we demand is simply part of the guarantee against violence and arbitrary interference.

If knowledge of the good were possible, then conscientious beliefs would not suffer from a cognitive inadequacy common to their kind, and the desirability of liberal institutions would not then be adequately explained by their freedom from the fictions which sustain traditional societies. But even in the absence of such knowledge, a clear dilemma frustrates any attempt to ground these institutions in demonstrable rights. Either these beliefs wrongly hold as true propositions which cannot be known or they make no claim to knowledge. In the former case they should lack the personal importance which makes liberal protections valuable. In the latter case they have a non-cognitive status which confines all political persuasions to the same plane. We may prize our moral convictions not for their assertive content but because they express adherence to a set of practices (keeping agreements, encouraging discussion, honoring one's parents, etc.). So understood, conscientious commitment can exist without assent to illusions, but this way of explaining the importance of conscientious beliefs is consistent with any number of ways of life – that of the caste, the tribe, the military, the monastery, and the diversity of other callings in which individual freedom has no central place.

This dilemma does not undermine the value of freedom of conscience for us. It simply shows that even this good should be understood as part of certain social arrangements. The desirability of such freedom can be supported, for example, by the benefits of diversity for modern societies, but the argument provides only indirect reasons for an individual right. If the practice of toleration and the institutions of a free press and scientific freedom are justified by their utility, then the rights they embed should certainly be observed. The epistemic criteria which distinguish the liberal theory of rights do not figure in this argument, however, and utilitarian justifications of liberal principles give them no permanent foundation. The utility of any institution depending upon contingent circumstances, the utilitarian mode of argument is politically and philosophically neutral. It can be as effectively employed by Burke as by Mill, both defenders of a particular way of life.[72]

These abstract reflections can be tested in a preliminary way by locating them in relationship to the educational theories and practices characteristic of Kohlberg and the Values Clarificationists. The crux of the argument is the distinction between the epistemological position that there is no truth in claims about good and virtue and the conception of conscientious convictions as adherence to certain practices. Suppose, then, that moral education properly rests upon the theory of value that denies truth to judgments about the good and thereby confines moral knowledge to abstract principles of choice. If knowledge is the aim of education, it follows that only these principles can be proper objects of moral instruction. It does *not* follow that the inculcation of ethical beliefs by public institutions is a violation of moral rights and freedoms, an invasion of privacy and conscientious belief. The violation of a right is a harm; but harm is done only when a good is attacked, and philosophical doubts about truth in matters of personal commitment can undermine the goods of privacy and freedom of conscience. If the epistemological tenet is correct, then moral beliefs below the level of principles can be deemed undesirable by rational individuals. This will emerge later as a particular problem for Values Clarification. Even so, the liberal freedoms may remain. In the absence of acceptable standards of evaluation, no interest is superior to any other. Consequently, no persons may justifiably impose their wills or values upon others who object to this subordination. If this means that the individual personality consists only in a collection of logically arbitrary preferences and sentiments, it does not negate the practical point that even human beings without character may wish to be free from interference and indoctrination.

Suppose now that moral education rests more comfortably on custom than on theories of knowledge and morality. Liberal qualms about indoctrination remain fully justified if the prevailing customs are traditions of freedom that make sense for pluralistic societies in which diverse moral and religious practices exist in addition to the arguments occurring within any particular practice. The absence of a common conception of the morally and religiously good life rules out any valid public preference for one set of moral and religious practices over another. It does not at all rule out insisting that certain liberties are goods and teaching that voting in elections, taking part in voluntary associations, enjoying consitutional protections, and participating in moral and religious practices are parts of well-being in a culture whose political traditions are liberal. These traditions define an area of general agreement on the good which exists in spite of disagreements elsewhere, and schools are legitimately structured to encourage the appropriate habits of participation.

There is another aspect of well being in a liberal culture. North Americans and Europeans have a valid interest in their separate identities and the independent pursuit of goals they have decided for themselves, but this too is a social way of life. It is not in any obvious sense an alienated existence but our peculiar mode of relationship. It does not discourage the development of character, since it promotes the moral qualities, the virtues, which constitute character – including prudence, justice, courageous responsibility for one's own circumstances and destiny, and charitable acceptance of moral ambiguity. It is only in promoting a view of freedom which is expressed in terms of abstract human rights rather than concrete customary expectations that we encourage an idea which raises individual separateness into a serious plight. What deprives individuals of the standards against which character can be measured is not the liberal virtue of independence but the metaphysical picture of personality as composed of arbitrary preferences ideally formed under the protection of "human rights" or the "moral law."

Liberal moral educators seldom reach this impasse, since at crucial moments theoretical argument is abandoned for the practical pursuit of common ideals. The history of Kohlberg's educational recommendations illustrates this irrelevance of theory to practice very nicely. When he defended the attainment of principled forms of moral reasoning as the proper objective of moral education, he argued that this objective alone "does not entail the violation of the child's moral freedom, which is involved in any other formulation of moral education's goals."[73] More recently, with growing realization that schools do not succeed in teaching a morality of principle, he has become convinced that educators must use an "indoctrinative" and "participatory" approach whose aim is "commitment to being a good member of a community or a good citizen." Otherwise "a person ... is unlikely to be in a position to have the capacities and motivation to enter positions of participation and public responsibility later."[74] The second of these positions could almost be an expression of Oakeshott's view of moral education as "the handing on of knowledge of how to behave" and his idea that "what has to be learned is not an abstract idea ... but a concrete, coherent manner of living in all its intricateness."[75] How, though, are we to reconcile respect for the child's moral freedom with indoctrination in the liberal value of participation?

There is no necessary relationship between the value of freedom and the value of participation in social life. The connection has to be drawn, and it can take one of two forms. If one accepts Kohlberg's epistemological principles the value of participation must be represented as extrinsic: without such involvement, he says, moral growth will be ended prematurely, since "development ... cannot take place except in and through experiences of participation."[76] In other words, if one values the moral autonomy which is the end of development, then participation is to be encouraged as the means to this end. Unfortunately, it cannot be justified in this way. Since participation does not lead to the philosophically principled level of morality, we lack evidence that engendering habits of democratic citizenship is even a necessary condition of development.

If, however, one accepts the view that moral learning in a liberal society leads to knowledge of how to behave, then participation should be understood as inherently desirable. Participation is part of the liberal way of life and moral freedom cannot be properly exercised apart from it. Educators animated by commitment to pluralistic culture can join in the battle against privatism, but their doing so requires no appeal to a liberal psychology of the individual and need not create disharmony between freedom and indoctrination. Moral freedom is absorbed within democratic practices and lacks the primacy of place from which it once seemed possible to justify those practices.

The consistent practical thread in Kohlberg's work is his insistence that education should be organized along democratic lines. Discussions of moral problems, it seems obvious to him, can foster moral development only in a social atmosphere which encourages taking other persons' points of view, and his basic point is not controversial. The understanding of others' expectations which is a precondition of appreciating a tolerant and egalitarian way of life is itself possible only if one has a sense of effective intercourse with one's associates, a capacity to influence and to be influenced by discussion. The atmosphere of discussion presupposed by the critical analysis of moral dilemmas is simply a climate in which energetic teachers communicate human purposes, foster solidarity, and treat students with respect. This is a formula for successful education of any kind, and the assumptions of liberal theory are largely irrelevant to it. Hence, in practice, Kolhlberg notes, "there is very little new in this – or in anything else we are doing."[77]

The philosophical theory through which Kohlberg interprets his findings in moral psychology is distinct from his educational practices,[78] and his account of "the freedom and rights of the child" only gets in the way of instilling the responsibilities of citizenship and the social meanings which are necessary for individual well being. This is why the theory is often tacitly ignored, especially when it would make apparent infringements of freedom difficult to justify. Few liberals consider it wrong to promote dispositions of participation even though it would seem a questionable intrusion from the standpoint of the liberal philosophy of rights. It is when viewed as an expression of the liberal tradition that the inculcation of such habits is innocent. The tradition needs no foundation and has none. It may be more defensible without one.[79]

The conservative conception of moral education places the liberal form of education within one set of cultural practices, and it lends itself to a more generous interpretation of the scarcity of moral agreement than seeing moral beliefs as dubious cognitive states. These beliefs seem better viewed in terms of participation in local social practices than as propositions which can command universal agreement, and the second account thus stands free from the epistemological assumptions typical of recent liberal philosophies of education. It lends itself rather to an honoring of one's cultural traditions and to recognition that liberty is not a simple state of being but a complex and changing cluster of rightful expectations. The cluster familiar to us defines the liberal conception of liberty, but relevant expectations exist wherever there are practices which include filial, political, cultural, legal, religious, and moral ways of relating to other people. It is in mastering them that we come to prize the opportunities and honor the obligations they include. Liberal institutions are one important expression of these needs. For most of us who have been raised in this tradition, no other way of life is likely to be desirable or even possible, and this way of life must be learned like any other. If those like Hampshire, Oakeshott, Rorty, and Walzer are right, this learning has nothing to do with philosophical theories and everything to do with mastering a set of practices.

A great deal remains to be said about these practices and their defensibility. To forsake philosophical theory leaves them without any stated means of justification against opposing cultural currents. This situation can be discomforting and easily encourages reversion to theory in protection of our conscientious commitments. To make this move, on the view described here, is unwarranted, but the problem it expresses is real. No one who prizes liberal institutions will be content to say, "this is what we do," but must want the means of safeguarding the cultural heritage.

From the anti-theoretical perspective of our modest moral conservatism, the answer to this problem has two main parts. They are elaborated in the next two chapters. One part is an account of the good life which identifies a set of natural moral agreements. This will not be a philosophical account of human nature; it will not justify these agreements by reference to some permanently valid or external standard. On the contrary, it will show why the structure of basic natural agreements makes it inevitable that they will be overlaid by disagreements. At the same time it will help give definition to the exercise of hermeneutic sensitivity, critical reflection, and related capacities needed if disagreements are to be resolved through something – the second part – called the education of emotions.

Chapter 2

The Good Life

I A Developmental Story

Any understanding of moral education reflects views of human nature and development, of the innate potentialities which a child can be brought up to realize. To believe that members of modern societies cannot gain knowledge of the good is to suppose that moral knowledge can extend no further than the rational principles of choice debated by moral theorists. To take seriously the idea that relative strangers can reach agreement on a conception of the good life is to entertain the possibility that moral knowledge is more available than modern philosophers suppose.

The difference between these conceptions is especially clear in their political dimension. Everyone agrees that moral educators properly aim at enabling individuals to live a good life, but the dominant school of thought about human well being is part of the political theory "that government must be neutral on what might be called the question of the good life .... [P]olitical decisions must be, so far as possible, independent of any particular conception of the good life, or what gives value to life. Since the citizens of a society differ in their conceptions, the government does not treat them as equals if it prefers one conception to another."[1] The implication for public authorities is a certain disinterest in the aims of students.[2]

This neutrality is appropriate only in so far as we lack knowledge or simply disagree about the good. To be neutral is to be unaligned with any of the parties in a dispute, and to the extent that a consensus exists on important matters no violation of neutrality is involved in preferring one position over other conceivable ones. Where a community exists, students may be initiated into its culture – including its customs and values – and the very existence of public institutions of education rests upon some agreements of this kind.[3] It is important to know how wide they actually are and how wide they might become.

The uncertainties of moral education inherent in modern society make it unlikely and probably undesirable that any familiar conception of human well being should achieve a definitive victory over any other. Many of these uncertainties are present in Rousseau's story of *Emile*, but his account also includes all of the elements needed in order to describe a version of the Aristotelian conception of the good which is compatible with the realities of modern society. In his masterpiece on education, Rousseau struggled with the moral perplexities of modernity more successfully than many do today, and his animus against public education rested on an evaluation of his society rather than on a doctrine of what "government must be."

Emile's moral development occurs in stages. They are defined by modes of practical reasoning which succeed one another according to a pattern fixed by nature. It is part of the concept of a stage that one cannot properly understand claims representing a higher stage than one's own. In seeking to "indicate the order and development of our feelings and our knowledge in relation to our growth," Rousseau insists, for example, that "the child cannot ... know what he is doing when he makes a promise ... and when he breaks his promises he does nothing contrary to his stage of reasoning."[4] That feelings as well as knowledge must be examined is a central feature of Rousseau's story, distinguishing it sharply from developmental accounts supported by modern moral theory. While there are impressive descriptive similarities between Rousseau and Kohlberg in particular, they differ markedly in the explanations they offer. The role of feelings in *Emile* places it in a theoretical and philosophical tradition alternative to that of Kant, Mill, Dewey, and Rawls in which most moral educators now put themselves.

In the initial stage of rational development "the moral lessons which are and can be given to children may be reduced to this formula:

> Master: You must not do that.
> Child: Why not?
> Master: Because it is wrong.
> Child: Wrong! What is wrong?
> Master: What is forbidden you.
> Child: Why is it wrong to do what is forbidden?
> Master: You will be punished for disobedience.
> Child: I will do it when no one is looking.
> Master: We shall watch you.
> Child: I will hide.
> Master: We shall ask you what you were doing.
> Child: I shall tell a lie.
> Master: You must not tell lies.
> Child: Why must I not tell lies?
> Master: Because it is wrong, etc.

That is the inevitable circle. Go beyond it, and the child will not understand you."[5]

Young children, this dialogue implies, have no concept of right and wrong and can only understand the words in terms of punishment and obedience. Rousseau therefore advises that children be spared a lesson in misunderstanding, asserting that they should "find ... necessity in things, not in the caprices of man" which simply teach "deceit, falsehood, and lying as a way to gain reward or escape punishment."[6] He also observes, however, that this counsel is never heeded and that fear of punishment typically provides our initial construction of moral utterances.

In adolescence, Rousseau notes, foresight begins to develop and the child's natural restlessness turns into "curiosity about all things far or near which may affect himself" and "this curiosity ... is the means of development for the age with which we are dealing ... The innate desire for comfort and the impossibility of its complete satisfaction impel him to the endless search for fresh means of contributing to its satisfaction." The child thus becomes "a worker and a thinker" and "knows the essential relations between men and things but nothing of the moral relations between man and man ... He values most the things which are of use to himself, and ... never departs from this standard of values ... He thinks not of others but of himself, and prefers that others should do the same. He makes no claim upon them and acknowledges no debt to them ...." There is, however, recognition "that to get tools for his own use, other people must have theirs, and that he can get in exchange what he needs and they possess."[7]

At puberty, Rousseau's youth feels the stirrings of social sentiments. "His imagination is kindled by the first beginnings of sensibility, he begins to perceive himself in his fellow creatures, to be touched by their cries, to suffer in their sufferings ... So pity is born, the first relative sentiment which touches the heart according to the order of nature." With this new consciousness of relationship to others, this ability to "go beyond ourselves," one acquires the capacity for friendship, and "we have reached the moral order at last."[8]

Emile's "second step towards manhood" occurs when "convention ... has not yet made him its slave" and "He cares nothing for the weight of popular opinion, though he loves to give pleasure to others ... Hence he will be affectionate rather than polite." At the same time, "he will be delighted to gain approval" from his fellows. Regarding those who share a "taste in morals" he will think, "I am delighted because they say I have done right ...; while they judge so wisely it is a fine thing to win their respect."[9] But standards adequate for dealings with family and friends are not sufficient to decide questions of right and wrong. As Rousseau notes, "Emile is ... a member of society, and must fulfill his duties as such. He is made to live among his fellow men and he must get to know them." He "has now to learn how men live in the world."[10]

The morality of association is commonly followed by a morality of authority, and delight in the approval of one's friends is subordinated to respect for public opinion. Rousseau recognizes a law of conventional prejudice or opinion, such that "honor does not depend on ... conduct alone, but on ...reputation."[11] There are complications to be noted here however. As if in anticipation of Gilligan's identification of sexual differences in moral development, Rousseau distinguishes two alternative perspectives at this stage, one appropriate for men and one appropriate for women. In the same way that pity introduces us to the moral order, it is love which brings us to "the last act of youth's drama." Sexual passion propels us into the wider society in which differences between the genders have important moral implications. Intercourse has fateful consequences for women but not for men. The preservation of the family requires both that a mother be faithful to her husband and that he believe in her fidelity, but it places no corresponding constraint upon the man. Hence, "A man has no one but himself to consider, and so long as he does right he may defy public opinion; but when a woman does right her task is only half finished, and what people think of her matters as much as what she really is ... 'What will people think' is the grave of a man's virtue and the throne of a woman's."[12]

Rousseau's sexism should not be allowed to obscure an important qualification: "For all mankind there is a law anterior to that of public opinion ... This law is our individual conscience,"[13] which is the voice of natural inclination. The sentiment of love introduces duties to one's beloved, and because these may conflict with conventional prejudice it is possible in principle to distinguish the standard of right from social obligation. Ideally, Rousseau thinks, these two laws will be in harmony, in which case a morality of social authority is right for women – although he acknowledges the possibility of circumstances which erode the social differences between the sexes and lead to the disappearance of a double standard. Women may come to enjoy the freedom of men, or men may adopt a morality of authority. Either event he regards as a departure from the desirable course of development; but as we will see he also believes this conventionality to be a secondary rather than defining feature of the morality whose real standard is love. Understanding this difference will help to explain the appearance of sex-linked patterns in moral development and to see that their sexist implications can be avoided.

In the first two stages of development, Emile "has considered himself in his physical relations to other creatures," and, in the second two stages, "in his moral relations with other men." Now "there remains to be considered his civil relations with his fellow citizens." Emile's business is not "to pay court to those in authority but to establish the rights of humanity" and "the principles of political law" against which to measure "the positive laws of settled governments." Further practical understanding thus requires learning politics and realizing that legitimate government depends upon a hypothetical social contract in which each individual agrees with every other to form a legislative power wherein self-government establishes their freedom from any external authority. For one who reaches this level, "the public good, which to others is a mere pretext, is a real motive for him. He learns to fight against himself and to prevail, to sacrifice his own interest to the common weal. It is not true that he gains nothing from the laws; they give him courage to be just, even in the midst of the wicked. It is not true that they have failed to make him free; they have taught him to rule himself."[14]

Whether Emile's political education represents an additional stage of moral development is an important but difficult question. The reasons for thinking that it does not mark a new stage are best considered against the alternative account of development introduced by Kohlberg. This is the subject matter of chapters 4 and 5. Here it is enough to preview a second disagreement arising from Rousseau's important assumptions about the mechanism of development. Rousseau understands moral development as largely dependent upon a biological clock which is responsible for the emergence of a series of new attitudes. The clock can run fast or slow, for "the change from childhood to puberty is not so clearly determined by nature that it varies according to individual temperament and racial conditions" and "is always more precocious among educated and civilized races, than among the ignorant and barbarous."[15] Whenever it happens, though, the transition to stage 2 requires the newly formed capacity for curiosity, stage 3 must await feelings of pity, and stage 4 begins with love. Thus, in Rousseau's view, important aspects of the development of practical judgment must be explained in terms of these affective presuppositions.

Sentiments, in Rousseau's view, include standards of evaluation. When children become curious, the need for knowledge characteristic of the attitude provides a criterion for distinguishing desirable from undesirable behavior. Only actions which respect the truth are warranted, since ignoring evident realities is inconsistent with the desire to know. When pity arises, the need to comfort the suffering establishes the inherent value of other creatures as a criterion of judgment and right action superior to their instrumental value for oneself. The standard of lovers similarly requires them to honor the objects of their emotion. The fact that there are such standards entails that "the eternal laws of nature and order exist. For the wise man they take the place of positive law; they are written in the depths of his heart by conscience and reason."[16]

This is antique philosophy, but the point it makes is simple. The affective states marking the stages of individual growth include generalizable judgments of value: seek the truth; comfort the suffering; honor excellence. The attitudes which define and determine developmental stages cannot be correctly understood in abstraction from these intrinsic judgments, so that while the content of ideas of significant truth, undue suffering, and excellence may be influenced by social circumstances, the forms of judgment are universal. That is to say, it may be partly in terms of prevailing social expectations that we distinguish trivial from interesting truths, acceptable from excessive suffering, and real from imagined superiority; but the intellectual structure of our moral instincts does not vary.

Rousseau's eternal moral laws are not those of moral theorists. They are psychological, not philosophical truths. Their connection with naturally arising emotions explains our basic moral beliefs but it does not justify them. We have here a partial description of the origins of moral beliefs but nothing that provides a rational foundation for these beliefs. Although this is a non-normative conception of human nature, however, it describes normative judgments in a way which permits them to be rationally justified. In so doing it provides the essential element which will eventually permit the conservative conception of moral philosophy to incorporate an acceptable account of justification for our practices.

II Emotional Goods

If Emile's story is taken seriously, then the prescriptions of the received view of public education neglect one important fact. While our particular aims may differ, we nevertheless share an abstract idea of the good life. Individual conceptions of the good are various, but we agree on the elements of the concept of the good and only interpret it in a number of ways. To experience curiosity, pity, and love is to feel a need to gain knowledge, to diminish suffering, to possess something good. The feelings thus establish crucial purposes, and to be thwarted in the pursuit of these goods diminishes our well being.

This agreement is far denser than the sentiments which define the stages of Emile's development. We all experience many passions which are connected with insistent desires and also with judgments which when correct justify the desires, making them rational desires. These feelings are not inscrutable impulses which simply assail us but cognitive-affective states which link desires with reasons for them.

In this, Rousseau did not differ importantly from the classical tradition. Plato aligned emotions and their concerns with reason and against appetite; and Aristotle identified virtues by reference to the passions, thus bringing both feeling and behavior under cognitive scrutiny. Within this conceptual scheme, the urge to know can be regarded as a rational desire: curiosity is aroused by unusual events and warranted by the fact that novelty justifies this curiosity. The desirability of knowledge is thus distinguishable from a simple hunger for learning and from the mere usefulness of certain sorts of information. In the same way, fear and the desire for safety aroused by the appearance of danger are justified if the danger is real; and pride and the associated desire for recognition, are justified by significant accomplishments. Only curiosity, fear, and pride which are not proportionate or appropriate to their objects lack good reasons according to this ancient view.

In order to be clear about this class of rational values, it is useful to see how all of the items on a long list of passions display an identical structure of judgment and desire which distinguishes emotional goods from instrumental goods and the objects of non-rational urges:

When we admire things or persons we judge them to be somehow excellent and wish to emulate, honor, or defer to them.

In anger we judge something to be an offense and desire to punish the offender.

Awe comes from the perception of something sacred or mysterious, and it engenders the desire to honor or worship it.

Guilt arises from knowingly violating others' rights or failing in one's responsibilities, and it includes an interest in making amends.

Pride is tied to the judgment that one has accomplished something and to a desire for recognition.

Respect involves understanding that one has equals and makes us want not to sacrifice their interests to our own.

Sadness results from a perception of loss and arouses the desire to recover the missing thing.

In trust one believes that a person will behave as expected and desires that the person be dependable.

This is only a small fragment of a full "register of emotions," as Robert Solomon has called such lists. They were once standard in moral philosophy. Historically important ones appear in Hobbes's *Leviathan*, Spinoza's *Ethics*, Smith's *Theory of Moral Sentiments*, and Hume's *Treatise*. That they have largely ceased to compel attention is a measure of the decline of philosophical interest in virtues and the good. Their disappearance does not, though, necessarily reflect a weakened sense of well being, habits of the heart being stronger than the ability of modern civilization to sever unions of reason and desire.

Articulating the surviving sense of well being will be easier if we keep it in mind that even this sample of the set of rational attitudes shows our common concept of the good to be extremely multifarious. The diversity of emotional goods – intellectual, physical, social, religious, moral – displays the richness of our rational aspirations. It also suggests that it would be inappropriate to isolate any sort of evaluation and to treat it as especially important or distinctive, and the point is reinforced by the structural identity of the family of attitudes in question. Moral feelings like pity and respect do not manifest a peculiarly moral form of reasoning, since all of the above judgments display the same formal relationship to the attitudes they define and to the needs which follow from their validity.

Moral judgments are ordinary, but moral philosophers and educators often regard them as unique and sui generis. Kohlberg observes that if we "make no direct claims about the ultimate aims of people, about the good life, or about other problems that a teleological theory must handle," then questions of good will move "beyond the scope of the sphere of morality."[17] This opinion well reflects one consequence of philosophical uneasiness about the concept of well being. By supposing that emotional purposes lack validity one becomes unable to

48

identify rational conceptions of the good life. Disputes about desirability then appear intractable unless moral reasoning is severed from other forms of purposive deliberation and put above them as an impartial adjudicator. As a result the scope of morality and moral education contract to the search for formal principles of adjudication between competing interests.

Against the background of these philosophical assumptions, it is surprisingly easy to identify the primary constituents of the many other common feelings – such as contempt, gratitude, hate, hope, humility, indignation, jealousy, resentment, shame – which include rational ends. Where it is not easy to make such an identification a simpler passion is likely to be under consideration. Empathy resembles pity in being a form of distress which is evoked by another's distress, but it makes no judgment about the degree or deservedness of the other's suffering and is only an egoistic response to it.[18] Joy, too, can be contrasted with simple pleasure, hatred with mere aversion, love with attraction. However for most purposes this sorting into kinds is not necessary. That would be required only if one wanted to insist that every occurrence of real pity, for example, has a judgment attached. To the contrary, each recognized emotion is a family of responses, and a characteristic judgment defines the family rather than each of its members. Not everything we call "pity" exhibits all the features of judgment and desire which make up the intellectual and purposive structure of a complex emotion.

Love provides an interesting test for the claim that every emotional family is defined by a characteristic judgment. In contrast to fear, which we assess in terms of fairly well-recognized dangers, love seems to resist the agreed-upon criteria of evaluation which are needed if an opinion is to be regarded as true or false.[19] Love, it is sometimes said, does not characterize its object. Being inspired by qualities which are appreciated only by the lover, there is no clear public test of its appropriateness; the emotion's intellectual structure is not complemented by definite judgmental content. However, without pretending that any short discussion can deal adequately with this subject of universal interest, we should note that "love" is a general word which is applied to a variety of states, some of them lacking the typical structure of emotions, others lacking testable judgments, still others exhibiting both desire and judgment. Fondness and affection stand to complex forms of love as empathy to pity, being responses which raise no questions of evaluation. Sexual love consists in what Rousseau called the "physical element" in the complex emotion, in contrast to the moral element which ascribes such qualities as beauty to its object.[20] Infatuation is foolish love, recognized only because we regard the evaluation it makes of its object as lacking in judgment. In making these discriminations, an emotion comes into focus which is supported by beliefs about one's lover's virtues: Emile's desire for sexual intercourse becomes love when his ideal of Sophie becomes inseparable from his lust. Her virtuous qualities do justify an emotion and increase the satisfactions of an affectionate liaison. This form of love is fully analogous to the fears aroused by impending injury, loss, difficulty, or suffering. Because it reflects a course of learning it also constitutes an appropriate aspiration of moral educators.

Various retrospective attitudes are test-cases for the claim that emotions display desire or purpose. Regret and sadness do not appear to include a want but only the wish that things had been otherwise. What is done, after all, cannot be undone, so that regret is not tied to remedial action and is not a strongly practical attitude. Nonetheless, it is one of our measures of the genuineness of regret that a person be concerned to avoid circumstances which may make regrettable actions unavoidable. Regret is intertwined with prudence, since a person who was never concerned about future harms would not have reason to take them seriously after the event. Sadness, too, has a practical aspect, since losses may be recovered. Grief stands out as purposeless, but because it is appropriate only when there is nothing to be done any practical desire would fly against the facts. Joy, too, may include no purpose when it is aroused by a happy accident but, like grief, is intelligible only within a framework of purposes. It may be the outcome of successful struggle for something desirable, just as grief may result from misfortune in endeavor as well as through bad luck. In this broader sense there are no clear counter-examples to the statement that emotions are expressions of desires.

To the extent that particular instances of emotions lack the desire-belief structure, a broadly teleological account of the good life requires amendment. Life includes good luck and misfortune as well as intentions. This by no means detracts from the fact that the passions which exhibit this structure include rational purposes. In conferring meaningfulness upon our desires, emotions establish an essential part of human well-being. We justifiably feel unhappy when these purposes are frustrated. Moreover, the things we want most can be traced to these emotionally determined purposes. Not desires in general but those which demand justification define the most important condition of human happiness. They define a structure of needs that gives each human life a common shape and a dimension it would not have if we were motivated only by simple appetites and affections which lacked internal elements, incorporated no judgments, and raised no questions of validity.

Needs are not simply subjective states, for we may not really need certain things which we feel we do; and we may need something of which we are unaware. These requirements are of several kinds. We have physical needs which must be filled if we are to survive and prosper. We also have instrumental needs – the necessary means to achieving other things we want or need. The needs of most interest here, however, are those which define the emotional purposes for which we have non-instrumental reasons. They are as vitally important as the minimal requirements of organic life or any technical imperative.

Emotional needs are rational ends, since the correctness of the judgments typical of these passions justifies their characteristic purposes. Once again, the urge to know is not an egoistic craving in persons who have tasted learning but a justifiable desire whose objectivity warrants terming knowledge a need. This objectivity does not reside in the demonstrable usefulness of certain sorts of knowledge but in the fact that the unexpected qualities of things inspiring curiosity justify the attendant desire to learn about them, as well in the fact that we can mistakenly ascribe interest to things which are not really worthy of study. (To find qualities unexpected may simply reflect unjustifiable ignorance.) The need to know is not an arbitrary wish or a utilitarian imperative, for it exists only if there are things worth learning about. Assuming that there are such things, we have reason to judge ignorance to be an unfortunate (though often unrecognized) state of deprivation.

To feel pity for persons is to judge them to be suffering some serious harm or injury and to wish to comfort them – a desire for which there is good reason if the judgment is correct. Real suffering gives beings capable of pity a need to intervene. The wish to help does not result from a quirk or calculation of essentially self-interested human beings but is an expression of justified fellow feeling. The needs for security and recognition are likewise rational interests whose satisfaction is a condition of human well being. They are not instrumental goods, for there is no independent end for which they are typically desired as means. They are not dumb cravings, for merely feeling safe and gaining reputation do not satisfy the demands of fear and pride, false security and undeserved recognition being worthless. We need security and recognition not when having them would provide subjective satisfaction but only when they reflect the reality of the situation. The good life is not a fool's paradise or a utility-maximizer's dream.

It is such needs which define the basic set of human interests and the framework of the good life. As human beings we share an emotional repertoire which imbues us all with the same kinds of needs and the same abstract concept of the good. Within this framework there is ample room for individual differences, and in this sense it is clearly true that individual conceptions of the good differ. We may wonder about different things and seek different kinds of knowledge. We may strive for achievement in different areas and expect recognition from different people. We may place different weights upon these and other goods, some of us having little interest in knowledge for its own sake, while others are strongly motivated by curiosity. Such variations occur, however, within the same structure of rational ends upon which everyone agrees and which defines a common idea of the good. Even those who do not seek knowledge can agree that it is a worthwhile object of endeavor.

Aristotle made these points about the value of knowledge when he said, "all men by nature desire to know." Much knowledge is sought for its own sake rather than for its usefulness – as is shown by the fact that it began to be pursued only after almost all the necessities of life had been secured.[21] But there is an important challenge to this claim about knowledge and by implication to the more general view of emotional purposes as rational ends. In contrast to Aristotle's view that what we want when we want knowledge is deep understanding of principles governing reality, Nietzsche claimed that our object is for "something strange to be reduced to something *familiar*." It is "the *instinct of fear* that bids us know."[22] The need for knowledge is thus the need for security rather than for truth.

The general problem raised by this suggestion is that emotional motivations may be rationalized only by mistaken claims. The connection between emotions and judgments is less open to cognitive scrutiny than an Aristotelian view of the good life implies, since the passions promote deep self-deception. But where exactly is the disagreement here, and where exactly the self-deception? Aristotle and Nietzsche agree on the central anti-rationalist point that the need for knowledge is tied to feelings of some kind, whether they be wonder or fear, and it is well known that these feelings are not always clearly distinguishable. They are closely connected in primitive societies, and the connection remains for us in feelings of awe, or fearful wonder.

It is interesting that the motives of security and knowledge are related in this way. The connection is consistent with the developmental progression in which curiosity emerges after and depends upon a capacity for fear. This does not show that emotional judgments are deeply deceptive. What the contrasting opinions confirm is that these judgments are in a sense fictive, not modes of representing reality but of interpreting it. Arguments will be offered in the next chapter for holding that our concepts for the objects of our attitudes are inherently evaluative and as such subject to continuing interpretation. The desire for security is justified if one's situation is genuinely dangerous, but which situations are those? People fear different things; different cultures find different things dangerous. Like Aristotle, we may fear death, but Homeric heroes did not. We fear poverty; for many people it is an accepted condition of existence. Danger, in short, is not an objective state if by that we mean something which exists independent of fearful attitudes. The desire for security, therefore, cannot be distinguished from other desires from some standpoint independent of our attitudes. Given that these attitudes themselves are defined by reference to certain judgments and desires, there is no deep or hidden sense in which judgments about novelty are really apprehensions of danger or desires for knowledge are really unacknowledged cravings for security.

The urge to know is justified when events are interesting, but which are those? The answer is peculiar to an individual's past experiences and a culture's history. Events which justify a child's interest may not be worth an adult's time. Many philosophers consider books on metaphysics to be contributions to knowledge; others think them only sophistry and illusion. What counts as knowledge is a matter of interpretation and is not in this sense an objective state. To this extent, to speak of a claim as "knowledge" is to dignify it as well as to describe it. There is no being systematically mistaken about knowledge except for supposing that all the disputes arising from this inherently contentious concept might be permanently settled. The important issue, therefore, is not the matter of possible self-deception, but how our purposes can survive a clear understanding of them as fictive in this way.

Before entertaining this question, the picture of the good life needs to be completed by elaborating one of the implications of contestability. In contrast to the "primary goods" postulated by Rawls (things which every rational person is presumed to want because they have a use no matter whatever else one wants),[23] the abstract goods of security, knowledge, etc., support no such presumption. Some of them a rational person may not much want, and when wanted they are usually wanted for their own sake rather than for their usefulness. Even then they are subject to disagreements from which primary goods should be immune. Because passional desires are subject to contention, interpretations of the abstract good diverge. This picture of the good life thus includes great room for conflict and diversity. This fact defines an important dimension of the good life in any society of reflective people and contributes enormously to the complexity and richness of human well being.

III Rights and conflicts

There are prejudices of instinct and prejudices of history. The first make it reasonable to speak of a single moral "form of life" constituted by the human propensity to make familiar emotional judgments. The second constitute a diversity of moral ways of life defined by different communities and their customs. Between such ways of life discourse may be difficult or "abnormal" in Rorty's sense, lacking in recognized criteria for arriving at agreements, but even within them these barriers can be serious. How do the painful conflicts which result affect this picture of the good life?

In many respects they enhance the picture by showing cultures as not frozen over. A conflict of interpretations is an important part of social solidarity in any but the most brittle traditional culture. Conflicts within society and the soul may be "the stuff of morality as we ordinarily experience it,"[24] but these are not always harmful or undesirable. If MacIntyre is right, we should hope for "just the right kinds of tension or even conflict, creative rather than destructive, on the whole and in the long run, between secular and sacred, local and national, Latin and vernacular, rural and urban." For "when an institution – a university, say, or a farm, or a hospital – is the bearer of a tradition of practice or practices, its common life will be partly, but in a centrally important way, constituted by a continuous argument as to what a university is and ought to be or what good farming is or what good medicine is. Traditions, when vital, embody continuities of conflict."[25]

Unless a society's practices are frozen over, competing interpretations of its intrinsic goods develop and parties contend for dominance. But if such competition is an important part of participation, the conflict is not fundamental. Just as both sides in a game share the desire that their opponents try to win, there is a complex mutuality within factional struggles which unites their interests. Even for the losers, the tension is a locus of meaningful activity which would not be available were there no conflict. Some people may remain disappointed or angry at the conclusion of such a contest, but it is arguable that they are done no harm. Their grievances are superficial in that the possibility of pursuing a cause successfully includes the chance that it will not prevail. This might be viewed as the moral analogue of theodicy. In the best of all possible lives competing interpretations figure prominently. Liability to moral loss and defeat is its unavoidable price.

Such conflicts presuppose a kind of agreement within communities, and, in virtue of being conflicts of emotional ideas, imply a certain agreement between groups as well. As long as people participate in the analogous institutions which enable them to enter into meaningful opposition at all, they share the abstract ideas of goods and purposes which define a common form of life. The suggestion that there is no basis for resolving conflicts between differing ways of life must be qualified accordingly. It cannot be rejected outright, since in arguments about purposes there is no required outcome. No path leads unfailingly from conflict to harmony. But this is true within communities as well, and in both cases some outcome may be possible. Debate may give an abstract idea a dominant concrete interpretation.

Many conflicts are not between interpretations of the same abstract goods but between competing ones, and here resolution may be even more difficult. When a desire for knowledge conflicts with proud religious doctrine, or when love of parents collides with respect for law, we have the unhappy stuff of competing inherent values. Are such problems simply nonsense, or must they be regarded as signs of deep difficulties of the sort reflected by the logical paradoxes arising within ordinary languages? Just as those paradoxes have no straightforward logical solution, the occurrence of moral dilemmas only shows that conflicts arise which have no solution of the sort dreamed of in rationalistic moral philosophy. But just as the logical paradoxes do not impair our ability to communicate, moral dilemmas do not frustrate the moral practices within which they arise.

The ideal of rationalistic moral philosophy is a social order in which conflicting demands are finally reconciled. Moral conservatism demurs. "We ought not even to expect that conflicts between moralities, which prescribe different priorities, will gradually disappear, as rational methods in the sciences and in law are diffused."[26] These conflicts can nevertheless be addressed philosophically. Moral conservatism rebuts rationalistic moral theory in such a way that implacable moral animosities must be viewed as irrational. They exist where competing certainties prevent continuing discussion, but modern moral conservatism has no room for certainties of this kind. Because moral judgments are expressed in concepts which are inherently contestable, they cannot claim indubitability. The abstract moral laws inherent in human emotions can hardly be questioned, but their application to concrete cases cannot occur apart from habits and inclinations which have no permanent validity. Philosophical reflection can thus yield legitimate commentary on the sad history of social conflicts and schisms resulting from the extremer divergences in the interpretation of goods which characterize any institution or people. It so doing it may have a role to play in moderating moral conflict.

Reflection shows that there is no sharp difference between basic moral dilemmas and the choices we often have to make between possible ways of life – choices which entail that we will be basically changed. Sartre's freedom fighter has to decide between a course of action which requires courage, violence, dedication, deceit, selflessness, and loyalty and another which calls for friendship and affection, gentleness, acquiescence in public injustice, and passivity in the fact of others' suffering. Neither is wholly desirable, and to achieve the one is to impair the other.[27] But these sacrifices cannot be clearly distinguished from those involved in the specialized lives of artists, athletes, politicians, or priests. They also occur in the lives of ordinary people and are a commonplace of the moral form of life. The modern mode of existence includes a vast range of choice amongst alternatives, but some desirable choices make others unavailable. The absence of rational solutions to such conflicts between (and within) ways of life is consistent with the rationality of the end chosen.

The intrinsic connection between a view of the good and the possibility of conflict defines a complementary dimension of moral importance. The role this account of the good life accords to rights distinguishes it sharply from the view standard in moral theories. Whereas the orthodox Kantian conception of morality places rights over conceptions of the good, this relationship is reversed here. If we do not view rights as following from our common humanity we will see them as an aspect of shared, local conceptions of social goods, as rightful expectations justified by custom. In contrast to unrepentant deontologists like Charles Fried, who maintains that it is precisely "our common humanity" on which rights are based,[28] Michael Walzer complains that we can find "less in a universalist conception of persons than in a pluralist conception of goods."[29] The deontological view bases rights upon a conception of rational agents who construct their own view of the good: rights exist to protect this possibility. Once goods are tied to social meanings, the individual does not have this original freedom. Goods are matters of local knowledge and debate rather than creations of individual choice, and attached to these goods are local rights which protect them.

A pluralist conception of goods also conflicts with any form of utilitarianism not vacuously endorsing "utility in the largest sense." The principle of utility incorporates the idea that there is one intrinsic good; it assigns this good priority over the concept of right and defines right in terms of the promotion of the good. If pleasure and happiness have many forms, however, utility provides no clear definition of this kind; and no common capacity for happiness can be identified which would give clear content to the notion of the greatest good for the greatest number.

This question aside, it is clear that insofar as goods are social goods, rights are local and particular. Goods are tied to social institutions whose rules define specific rights. The variability of these institutions includes the variability of the rights, which are subject to extension and restriction in ways familiar from the history of property, work, education and politics. Such rights are neither permanent nor universal but customary and conditional, resting upon specific understandings established over the evolution of the institution in question or agreed to during a period of reform – as tenure developed as a protection for the pursuit of knowledge practiced within the institution of education. They have no rationale apart from such practices. Goods thus have priority over rights.

The lessons of our feelings are universal aspects of being human, but not in being necessary parts of practical rationality. They express how the world is seen by any creature capable of fear, shame, resentment, and like sentiments, but we can imagine beings able to make plans and seek the good without suffering these particular passions. Distressing experiences at the sight of suffering would not afflict a pitiless observer, however skillful in applying abstract rational principles of utility or justice. Nor would such occurrences necessarily perturb a person whose traditions mandated acceptance of pain. The passions instruct reason only when conventions give them content. Natural sentiments establish laws of conscience, but these laws have practical application only when they gain particular meaning from customary institutions. Rational expectations then exist to test emotional responses for appropriateness.

Universal moral laws are not the principles typical of deontological and consequentialist views of ethics. Rules of justice do not occur apart from the affective judgments whose intellectual structure and conceptual content contain all that is permanent in moral rationality. Thus, resentment includes a perception of unfairness, and this judgment can be parsed in terms of equal treatment; but our interest in equality has no basis except our tendency to respond in certain ways to certain relationships. No independent principle is responsible; but none is needed, for requiring that equals be treated as equals is fully accounted for by the defining conditions of resentment. Nor do we need or have available a satisfactory account of rights as universal requirements of human nature. "Our common humanity" refers to nothing clear if it does not describe features of moral psychology common to all human beings, and universality in this sense is consistent with the contingencies of interpretation which explain why we have the particular rights we do – the concrete entitlements attached to any system of social meanings. These rights are goods rather than elements of a framework within which we pursue goods which exist independently of them. The contrary view – that there are universal human rights valid under any social circumstances – conflates a universalistic way of life with a set of supposedly universal moral requirements, subjecting a political tradition to a philosophical intuition.

Of course, the intuition questioned here is supported by arguments, past and present, meant to show that rationality supports a conception of morality as consisting in categorically binding requirements on all agents. Among the most recent and exemplary is Alan Gewirth's attempted derivation of basic rights and obligations from the existence of necessary goods. There will undoubtedly be more such attempts, but they are unlikely to be more convincing than Gewirth's, which rests on the contention that because a measure of freedom and well-being are conditions of rational action a rational agent must claim a right to them.[30] The difficulty for such arguments is that a needed entailment between the goods of freedom and well-being and the corresponding rights is invisible to careful and trained observers like MacIntyre and others.[31] An agent is not obviously being inconsistent in recognizing the goods but questioning a right to them, thereby blocking any further inference to human rights.

If belief in "rights of man" is better understood as the expression of a political way of life than in terms of a priori reflection, it is also better explained in this way than by accounts (like MacIntyre's) ascribing it to the decay of convention and conversation in modern society. We are amply bestowed with traditions. In our way of life individual autonomy and independence are important goods; our lives are poorer without them. Freedom is central to our mode of well being because it expresses a collective sense of rights and responsibilities appropriate in a culture that often finds agreement on specific values difficult. It is no less a collective sense for consisting of shared meanings which include rightful expectations about the separateness of persons and the pursuit of self-interest.

Insofar as there is agreement about the abstract purposes which characterize particular emotions, and insofar as rights arise as protections of these goods, certain abstract rights can be generally acknowledged. Because we experience fear, curiosity, pity, and love it is part of the good life for human beings to be free from danger, to gain knowledge, to give comfort and be at one with others. It is reasonable to expect people everywhere to claim a right to be secure, to learn, to help others and to form personal attachments. A community in which such rights did not exist in some form is hardly imaginable. But these are not human rights in the sense that they follow logically from conceptions of the good or in the sense that they protect certain

61

universal entitlements. The right to security may be expressed as a claim upon private property, upon social welfare, upon housing of a certain standard, upon nuclear armament or nuclear disarmament, or in a multitude of ways which differ enormously according to prevailing expectations. The right to learning may be the right to go to school, or the right to hunt with one's father, or the right to read books. No concrete right is universal. Even the right to life is qualified in a myriad of ways and may count for little if people are united in common pursuit of a higher purpose.

The texture of the good life is thus complex and flawed by conflict and by continual pressure on our rights. It is unimaginable as well as undesirable that individual lives should ever be free of these difficulties. This may seem a dangerous view, and it may actually be one, for there are also reasons for the appeal of human rights. Expectations are malleable, easily skewed by participation in racist company, engagement in wartime situations, and psychological experiments. Hatred, massacre, and insensitivity are all too easily generated by our company. Must we simply view such attitudes and behavior as reasonable and acceptable in their particular places, as part of the contestability of moral conceptions? Are there no grounds on which to defend contrary moral judgments? Do the flaws in the good life extend to conflicts between groups, and if they do is that not ample reason to dispense with the notion of the good life in favor of principles which guard our humanity?

In order to address such questions properly, we need a fuller sense of the critical possibilities of moral thinking. How exactly do our shared criteria of evaluation work in actual arguments? There are disagreements here as well. We contest what constitutes security; we also contest the conditions of successful agreement on these matters. Elaborating the competing conceptions of valid moral criticism is thus essential to understanding the structure and limits of moral and emotional knowledge. The main conceptions are three. Each corresponds to a conception of moral education, a conventional account to Oakeshott's, a critical account to Kohlberg's, a consensual account to Paulo Freire's. We want to determine the extent to which each serves a valid purpose. This initial epistemological inquiry will not be immediately concluded, but it will enable us to pursue the matter further in later chapters.

IV Moral validity

Let us take this for granted: in experiencing the moral attitude of guilt one believes oneself to have been dishonest, cruel, selfish, unfair, or otherwise to have acted wrongly. Our use of these concepts is not to be explained primarily by appeal to principles, as we have seen above. We need to avoid such actions because they conflict with moral well being, contrary to the idea that moral reasoning is adequately characterized as a mode of resolving conflicts of interest. A druggist who refused to provide medicine to save a dying pauper would be being selfish; under the circumstances the interest in profit is not simply outweighed by the interest of the other person, for selfish desires lack justification. This is not a case in which, after consulting a personal system of ends in the light of principles like the golden rule, one finds that one cannot conscientiously pursue a desire for profit. Possibly one could. The wish is indefensible independently of what the person in question may think or feel.

To call an action selfish is to say that it exhibits excessive self-interest. Settling a disagreement about the validity of the judgment requires having a dependable standard against which excess can be determined. To a first approximation, the standard we employ is provided by the set of mutual expectations generated in social life. These expectations identify the extent of normal self-interest and enable us to distinguish certain departures from this norm as selfish. In terms of the above example, our collective experience leads us to expect a claim to property to be subordinated to the claim to life, and we are able to determine that profiting at the expense of life is unacceptable.

These judgments express the prejudices of history. Traditional expectations provide initial criteria for discriminating real from apparent threats, acceptable from unacceptable suffering, etc. Although these judgments are so far unreflective, they are not necessarily absolute. They are consistent with recognition that, under different circumstances, prevailing expectations about people's behavior would have differed. Since it is conceivable that traditions of self-reliance and responsibility should be more firmly entrenched than in fact they are, we can imagine hyper-entrepreneurial environments in which one's refusal to forego profit for the sake of another person would not be considered unduly self-interested. On the contrary, to extend such charity might be humiliating and contrary to the well-being of its recipient. However this kind of possibility need not undermine confidence in the standard established by actually existing traditions of behavior. They are the ones which are important in our lives.

Even in our society, the judgment upon the self-interested druggist is only an initial position. It is not the druggist's fault if a person in need of medicine cannot pay for it, and we do not expect the business to suffer on that account. We may instead expect victims of illness to be protected by social insurance or other public institutions of medical treatment. A druggist's demand for fair compensation implies selfishness only if it includes a refusal to respond in an emergency.

There is clearly wide scope for skillful reasoning within this conventional conception of moral judgment. The point can be generalized to all emotional judgments, which share the logic of virtues and vices illustrated by selfishness. The conceptual structure supporting Aristotle's doctrine of the mean displays the centrality of judgments of excess and deficiency. To feel fear, anger, and pity "at the right time, with reference to the right objects, towards the right people, with the right motive, and in the right way, is what is both intermediate and best, and this is characteristic of virtue."[32] The intermediate or mean which defines an excellence or virtue is always subject to argument and can be settled only in practice.

Aristotle seems rightly interpreted here as recognizing a close connection between moral judgment and social norms. The natural sentiments are closely tied to customs and traditions, since in experiencing fear, anger, and pity we make the judgments of qualitative comparison which characterize the emotions. We master the comparative concepts essential for these judgments only with exposure to social norms and distinctions. While we do experience these passions prior to achieving such mastery, it is also the case that until we gain familiarity with the conventions our emotions lack rational restraint and can only be chaotic. These social norms are, in consequence, essential conditions of coherent experience and not standards distinct from it. They express a way of life rather than being alien impositions. Our attitudes thus properly include a high value being placed upon the traditions required for dependable standards of judgment, as well as upon the original home of these judgments – family and neighborhood – and the patterns of law and order which protect such institutions. Roger Scruton insists, "To participate in a common culture is therefore ... to be gifted with a certainty in one's feelings, a certainty which the uprooted, alienated, and disenchanted may not have had, and may not want to have."[33] On this interpretation of evaluative judgments this certainty is justified by the rational expectations made possible by social norms of appraisal.

The obvious shortcoming of this conception of rational agreement is its lack of resources for dealing plausibly with problems arising from aberrant or competing practices. One way of handling this difficulty would be to pursue Aristotle's analysis of excellence in terms of skills and functions, hoping to establish a standard stronger than practical agreement by appealing to the proper function of human beings. Unfortunately, there is no plausible account of what the function of a human being might be.[34] The appeal to nature is not without merit though. If we must have more than agreement Burke may give enough in reflecting on contempt for the traditions of the *ancien régime*. He asks, "Why do I feel so differently?" and answers "because it is *natural* I should; because we are so made as to be affected by [such] spectacles with melancholy sentiments ...; because in those natural feelings we learn great lessons; because in events like these our passions instruct our reason."[35]   As for Rousseau, the lessons of the natural feelings are constraints on disagreement, and they limit the apparent need to deal philosophically with divergent practices.

However divergences do occur. Burke's account gives us no means of assessing practices foreign to ours when they conflict with our moral intuitions, and it leaves our own judgments liable to uprooting. MacIntyre's reflections on the discontents of modernity imply the absence of any certainty on account of the decay of settled expectations and confident acceptance of traditions. We may be left with the abstract first principles and core precepts championed by conservative moral educators,[36] but they no longer have any practical application. The analytic truths that selfishness justifies guilt and misfortune warrants sorrow are trivial in the absence of any evidence able to compel judgment. The concept of the good becomes an inchoate universal, and grounds for saying that emotions can be educated or justified fall away. The distinction between justifiable and unjustifiable purposes – between rational and other ends – breaks down, or it becomes obviously relative to one's choice amongst parochial communities in which a conception of the good manages to survive the acids of contemporary civilization.[37]   Under these circumstances mastery of moral concepts is pretty precarious.

Philosophically expressed, these doubts suggest that the intellectual structure of emotions and talk of mastering emotional concepts are misleading. Contrary to the conventional understanding, the judgments characteristic of emotions do not ascribe qualities to the objects of emotion but rather express evaluations that even our neighbors need not share. There are no important logical constraints upon conceptions of the good defined by the concepts of selfishness, loss, accomplishment, danger, novelty, suffering, etc. Reflection rightly convinces us that no amount of suffering entails that the victim deserves pity, so that we may adopt the stoical conclusion that human beings are responsible for enduring distress without complaint. But reflection also shows that there is no amount of suffering so small that it cannot be considered excessive, and we may instead subscribe to the epicurean notion that all pain is unacceptable and should be eliminated. The same sort of argument shows that there is no adequate ground for pride: no neutral description of an action logically implies that it constitutes a significant achievement, leading to the judgment that all is vanity. But parallel reflections also show that there are no grounds for lowliness or humility. Since all passions are independent of the evidence in this way there are an infinite number of possible, but rationally groundless, conceptions of the good.[38]

For this critical understanding of emotional judgment, emotions may present a perspective, and we are free to accept it, but it cannot be regarded as valid in any stronger sense. Those moral judgments which are tied to emotions are not otherwise defensible. Once we move beyond the most stable forms of conventional life, moral knowledge dissolves and any conception of the good evidently lacks good reasons. As Williams observes, the use of "thick" concepts in a maximally homogeneous and minimally reflective "hypertraditional" society expresses moral knowledge insofar as people deploy these concepts carefully, use the appropriate criteria, and so on. This knowledge is a reflection of practices, part of a stable way of living rather than the content of assertions having general implications which might conflict with other possible moral claims. The picture changes if we see the members of this society as trying to state the truth about values; for their judgments then have extensive implications, which they have never considered reflectively, and we have every reason to believe that, when those implications are considered, the traditional use of ethical concepts will be seriously affected. Reflection disturbs, unseats, or replaces traditional concepts, so that in ethics reflection can destroy knowledge.[39]

This rumination lacks bite if further reflection can restore confident use of "thick" concepts. Philosophical reflection does disturb customary values by disabusing us about any logically sufficient connection between describable evidence and emotional judgment, but the fact that the evidence does not make the claim it supports logically certain is compatible with its giving reasons to agree that the claim is true. In arguing with one another, rather than engaging in private philosophical inquiry, we give reasons which sometimes prove conclusive in generating agreement about what we know. The critical interpretation of moral beliefs is very important, releasing imagination but encouraging skepticism. The appropriate response is to overlay imagination with conversation.

In a fine series of passages which have little to do with his utilitarianism (but much with his defense of liberal institutions), J. S. Mill noted that "truth for purposes of action" is founded upon "discussion and experience." Unless an opinion is "fully, frequently, and fearlessly discussed, it will be held as a dead dogma, not as a living truth," for "truth in the great practical concerns of life, is ... a question of the reconciling and combining of opposites."[40] The last notion is ambiguous. It might be construed as the balancing of interests in a compromise, but Mill's idea can also be connected with a conception of moral knowledge when it is interpreted as describing the development of a consensus or standard accepted at the end of a discussion. Debate can yield decisions which are the bases of rational expectations about behavior. These decisions then have a similar logical role to the traditions which in the conventional view provide clear standards of evaluation. Here reflection promotes practical convergence.

The capacity for consensus is well developed in the intimate spheres of association where shared experience makes decisive agreement possible. Among strangers compelling norms may be more scarce, but there is no evident limit on the capacity of discussion to generate such standards. Rational people seek reasons for their judgments; and, since the only undogmatic way to find them is to share one's ideas and experiences with others, we may strive for agreement through debate. In such conversation, disparate bodies of experience imaginatively converge and can thereby narrow differences of judgment about the objects of fear, pride, curiosity, pity, and respect. By building a common reality in this way, strong restrictions are placed upon the range of interpretations possible for appraisive judgment. Extreme positions are discouraged by the act of sharing viewpoints and information. The resulting expectations then exercise compelling constraints upon conceptions of the good.

Such agreements are described by Freire, Jürgen Habermas, and others. There are three conditions for arriving at them. One is that we share a concept of the good life. This is the condition satisfied by a common psychological heritage – the common structure of evaluation resulting from the need-defining attitudes. There is no reason to suppose that all intelligent beings will inhabit the same kingdom of ends, but a shareable conception of the good is a possibility for any rational beings with the same emotional capacities.

The second condition of purposive agreement is that we escape the baseless standards which sustain rigid ideals and suppress emotions inconsistent with them. This might happen when God's word is held to preclude scientific curiosity or when caste distinctions make ethnic pride impossible. So, too, in the case of conventional stereotypes which designate certain emotions as required in certain customary situations. Since doubts about such standards are part of the process which finds expression in the critical understanding of value judgments, this condition is generally met when that interpretation has become dominant over the conventional understanding. It is part of the capacity to reach a rational consensus on practical matters that people are prepared to question and modify any custom or the application of any emotional concept.

The third condition is that the free inquiry and discussion advocated by Mill and others take place. This is not the same as subjecting the rules of institutions to logical criticism. The critical view that no fundamental evaluation of purposes is possible may limit discussion by insisting upon a framework in which human aspirations are assumed to constitute only personal desires and choices. Free inquiry and discussion constitute an attempt to construct the rational purposes which the critical view rejects as impossible.

The outcome of such a constructive inquiry cannot be stated in advance. Since the cognitive elaboration and justification of our attitudes depends strongly upon circumstances, and since it is partly within human power to determine these circumstances, the identification of rational purposes depends upon contingencies of fact and decision which are subject to change. In this respect the consensual interpretation will see merit in a conception of moral education which stresses a process of inquiry rather than a permanent set of conclusions. It will also approve ideals of democratic and non-indoctrinative schooling. It will not, however, understand this approval to preclude inculcating recognized virtues, for virtues are not doctrines. The excellences are expressions of a way of life, without which no rational purposes are possible. Nor will the support for democratic schooling be understood to mean that we must refrain from criticizing an individual's interests in the name of personal freedom. On the contrary, we will question the assumption that "the purpose of democracy is to register the desires of people as they are, not to contribute to what they might wish to be."[41] A virtue of democracy is that it permits the construction of purposes which have a claim to validity which is not simply the demand of custom.

So far these intimations of moral epistemology build casually on the phenomenological account of moral judgment sketched above. To be philosophically persuasive they must be connected more systematically to the intellectual structure of emotions and the pattern of psychological development. In the course of establishing these connections, practical convergence can be tied to practical perception and to improvements of emotional vision that amount to moral education.

Chapter 3

Educating the Emotions?

I Some intuitive psychology

Among the promising philosophical options for understanding moral experience is exploring the affective perception of facts salient for action. Thus Martha Nussbaum's identification of "morally salient" images in Henry James's novel, *The Golden Bowl*, with objects of knowledge: "Moral knowledge, James suggests, is not simply intellectual grasp of propositions; it is not even simply intellectual grasp of particular facts; it is perception. It is seeing a complex concrete reality in a highly lucid and richly responsive way: it is taking in what is there, with imagination and feeling."[1]

Some common patterns of philosophical thinking assign emotions to ethics and sensations to epistemology, assimilate rationality to cognitivity, and place desire and belief in different systems. Nussbaum's view of "passional reaction ... as itself a piece of practical recognition or perception,"[2] invites us to reshape these patterns. A major problem for her view is the difficulty of differentiating it clearly from some contrary assumptions about emotional states, including those of Henry's brother, William. The author of *Varieties of Religious Experience* challenged his readers to conceive themselves stripped of emotion and to imagine the world *"as it exists*, purely by itself, without your favorable or unfavorable, hopeful or apprehensive comment.... No one portion of the universe would then have importance beyond another; and the whole collection of its things and series of its events would be without significance, character, expression, or perspective."[3] This statement ascribes a salience to emotions which is not immediately distinguishable from Nussbaum's gloss on moral fiction. That Nussbaum and William James do differ is an important reminder of ambiguities pervading analyses of affective states.

The way in which feeling and emotion force facts upon attention is often noted. It forms part of Ronald de Sousa's exploration of the biological point of emotions, when he suggests that "the function of emotion is to fill gaps left by (mere wanting plus) 'pure reason' in the determination of action and belief.... Emotions are determinate patterns of salience among objects of attention, lines of inquiry, and inferential strategies."[4] They determine what logic cannot, namely what to attend to and inquire about. Were we without emotion, rational belief and action would not be possible. Hence, as McDowell puts it, when someone takes a fact "to be the salient fact about the situation, he is in a psychological state which is essentially practical."[5]

How, though, are such states to be understood? Does or does not de Sousa's comment exhibit the problem which Sabina Lovibond states in the following way?: "It is really the segregation of 'reason' and 'sentiment', or 'reason' and 'passion', in the faculty psychology of the eighteenth century which has been perpetuated in the 'fact/value distinction' of modern analytical philosophy."[6] The gaps between want and reason are all too familiar. To take them seriously counts against any view of passional reaction as perception. McDowell again: "Although perceptions of saliences resist decomposition into "pure" awareness together with appetitive states, there is an inclination to insist, nevertheless, that they cannot be genuinely cognitive states."[7]

Resisting this inclination and promoting the possibility of "affective cognition" does not only offer an alternative to philosophical orthodoxy. It also has practical importance. Cora Diamond notes of Wordsworth's conception of his poetic practice that he believes that we have a capacity to respond with deep sympathy to the feelings of other people - that is, when they are moved by the "great and simple affections of our nature," "the essential passions of the heart." .... In a sense, someone who has not learnt to respond with the heart in such ways has not learnt to think .... Poetry then helps develop the heart's capacities that are the basis for the moral life by deepening our emotional life and our understanding of it.... [Encountering literature] is a kind of learning to think; it plays an essential role in the education of the emotions and in the development of moral sensibility.[8]

This implies a different view of moral education than one which supposes "that a moral view can be *presented* in literature but its critical evaluation must be carried out through argument."[9] We will see in the next chapter how close the latter view of moral education is to Kohlberg's, precisely expressing his avowed "interest in literature's role in education, in literature as stimulating moral development."[10]

The distinction between literary presentation and critical evaluation is part of a broader philosophical perspective which includes characteristic views of virtue, emotion, and judgment contrary to those of Nussbaum, Lovibond, and Diamond. Its proponents regard it is a more scientific view, but the full practical importance of the difference between the opinions lies in the way that a conception of scientific inquiry may presuppose a theory of value and thereby serve a questionable social purpose. Programs of moral education which depend upon this conception will then include a hidden curriculum no matter how successfully they avoid specific moral content. As George Grant has put their practical point, "At the heart of modern liberal education lies the desire to homogenize the world. Today's natural and social sciences were consciously produced as instruments to this end."[11] Leaving aside the conspiratorial claim, his statement accurately conveys how studies which aim at truth may acquire a second function also suggested by Roberto Unger's claim that "the first principle of liberal psychology states that the self consists of understanding and desire, that the two are distinct from one another...."[12]

73

It would be easy to misinterpret the objection. Any investigation of living things raises normative questions. The study of how organisms work requires discrimination between proper and improper function, hence between normal and deficient specimens.[13] That scientific inquiry unavoidably involves evaluations of this kind is of minor philosophical interest. A great deal more interesting is the suggestion that much of modern psychology is deeply infected by philosophical theory. One important sign of this is the general absence of systematic treatments of connections between rational and emotional behavior and of any inquiry into rational purposes which could accommodate an account of the good. Since moral evaluations cannot be validated through sense or reckoning, empirical science is neutral about ends, but this neutrality means not ruling out the possible validation of purposes through forms of inquiry dealing with the interpretation of behavior. It is regularly violated, as by Kohlberg when he seeks to avoid the "psychological mistake underlying the bag of virtues approach" to moral education, namely that "common sense tends to treat moral words as if they described reality." If we accepted a "bag of virtues" then,

> it is evident how we should build character. Children should be exhorted to practise these virtues and should be told that happiness, fortune, and good repute will follow in their wake; adults around them should be living examples of these virtues, and children should be given daily opportunities to practice them....

But

> The psychologist's objection to the bag of virtues is that there is no such thing. Virtues and vices are labels by which people award praise or blame to others, but the ways people use praise or blame towards others are not the ways in which they think when making moral decisions themselves.[14]

An identical view supports Thomas Szasz's opposition to confining people in mental hospitals:

[P]sychiatric and sociological descriptions frequently offer promotive statements in the guise of cognitive assertions. In other words, while allegedly describing conduct, psychiatrists often prescribe it. Calling a person mentally sick is an example: it asserts, or implies, that his behavior is unacceptable and that he should conduct himself in other, more acceptable ways.[15]

For Szasz it follows that each of us should be able to pursue our own "path to personal freedom."[16] For Kohlberg, as we have seen, we properly demand of any educational practice that it "not entail the violation of the child's moral freedom" and protect "the liberty and rights of the child" by ensuring that its moral principles are self-constructed. These can be powerful moral appeals. Everyone knows of abuses of psychiatry committed for reasons of state or the convenience of families unable to cope with troublesome members. Everyone knows of educational institutions which stifle growth by requiring uncritical conformity to arbitrary rules of behavior. But our moral reactions to such practices express our views of decent and acceptable behavior. They do not depend upon linguistic and philosophical analyses which deny that these views are "cognitive assertions" or "true or false in the cognitive-descriptivist sense."

Contrary to Kohlberg's claim that psychological facts count against the identification of virtues, the best empirical backups for his semantics of value are surprisingly weak. They consist of studies of interpersonal consistency in appraisal and studies emphasizing disconnections between rational and emotional response. The former are exemplified by a set of experiments conducted in the 1920's by H. Hartshorne and M. May. The results showed little consistency in ascriptions of altruistic and honest behavior and thus suggested that the character traits we call "virtues" are not describable features of persons or behavior but disguised prescriptions. Kohlberg has repeatedly referred to this study as his primary source of the psychological facts supporting the "praise-and-blame label" account. Recent reexamination of the evidence shows, however, that it cannot be put to this use.

The consistency earlier found wanting is present in the data, so that the only remaining support for "the psychologist's objection" is philosophical,[17] and the best explanation of that philosophical opinion is historical and social.

As earlier citations of Unger and Grant indicate, the notion that these semantic claims are scientifically supported is challenged by observers as diverse as critical theorists and followers of Leo Strauss. They agree that the vast expansion of knowledge in our era coincides with a dramatic contraction in the conception of knowledge.[18] A society organized around the marketplace requires a vigorous institution of technical knowledge, but moral knowledge is not useful here. The market operates on the law of responding to what people want or can be induced to want rather than what they should want. It does not distinguish rational desires from others. It does not bring the ends of action into question. To be sure, a great part of life – perhaps the greater part – lies outside the sphere of exchange, but insofar as the market is the main principle of a society's structural organization, the possibility of rational ends is contrary to the ideology of personal freedom. Practical reasoning thus reduces to technical reasoning, and the pre-modern conviction that some interests are worthier of pursuit than others is replaced by the idea that interests are fundamentally unquestionable, hence appropriately modelled on bare likes and dislikes. Significant practical questions can then only be raised about the means to their satisfaction, and the good life can only be understood as the successful quest for whatever one happens to want. John Macmurray comments, "our lives belong to a stage in human development in which reason has been dissociated from the emotional life and is contrasted with it. Reason means to us thinking and planning, scheming and calculating."[19] It is not that we are stuck at the stage of adolescent Emile but that we understand our moral sentiments as solely passionate rather than rational.

The philosopher who has articulated this development most shrewdly is probably John Dewey. Dewey maintained that when we speak of "learning from experience" and the "maturity" of an individual or a group ... we mean that in the history of individual persons and of the human race there takes place a change from original, comparatively unreflective, impulses and hard-and-fast habits to desires and interests that incorporate the results of critical inquiry. When this process is examined, it is seen to take place chiefly on the basis of careful observation of differences found between desired and proposed ends (*ends-in-view*) and attained ends or actual circumstances.[20]

In immature states, according to Dewey, we experience numerous impulses which we indulge indiscriminately, but the resulting penalties and frustrations lead us to begin selecting among these impulses and modifying our actions. Through a process of deliberation in which various unreflective desires are weighed in terms of possibilities for realizing them, the "earlier impulsive tendencies" are "shaped into a *chosen* desire."[21] The long-term result is a deliberately fashioned system of desires and interests which is reasonable in having been constructed in the light of existing possibilities and resources for action.

Dewey well represents the mainstream of modern philosophy in identifying a class of reasonable interests which are distinct from the objectively rational interests that were supposed to exist by ancient philosophers. Such rational desires defined a structure of motivation which gave two tasks to practical reason. Given that we have certain ends or interests, we should inquire into the best means for achieving those ends; but we should also seek to ensure that the ends themselves are actually desirable. Dewey's reasonable desires lack this separate dimension. They are reasonable in resulting from reflective inquiry and reasoned choice, that is from considerations such as the probability of their satisfaction, their compatibility with feelings present in primary experience, and the like. No primary or underived desires are themselves subject to justification, however, for desirability is defined by instrumentalist reasoning alone.

Dewey does enrich his account with reference to the importance of feelings which "give us our *sense* of rightness and wrongness, of what to select and emphasize and follow up, and what to drop, slur over and ignore, among the multitude of inchoate meanings that are presenting themselves."[22] The reasonable interests are formed through inquiry which is based upon emotionally-charged sense and guided by means-ends reasoning. But while emotions are grounds of choice they appear in Dewey's view as "animal-like preference[s]" rather than as amenable to reflective inquiry.[23] For Dewey reasonable interests rest firmly upon non-rational individual feelings. No needs of the kind typical of the conception of the good life in chapter 2 are recognized within this view.

The same care is required in stating this case as in interpreting the difference between Henry and William James on emotional perception. It is possible, with Rorty, to compare Dewey's *Human Nature and Conduct* and Heidegger's *Being and Time* as both offering a moral psychology which avoids oppositions between "preference" and "reason,"[24] but their understandings of the matter are as instructively contrasted. Dewey's point is that impulsive desires are shaped into desires which contain reasons as the result of means-ends inquiry. Reflective desires are derivative from naive impulses. This account accepts the distinction between reason and desire at the basic level. By contrast, phenomenologists like Heidegger and Max Scheler express a view reminiscent of Nussbaum, Diamond, and Lovibond. Scheler criticizes the "prejudice [which] consists in upholding the division between 'reason' and 'sensibility'" – a division which demands that "our *whole emotional life* ... be assigned to 'sensibility.'"[25] Heidegger rejects this prejudice in maintaining that affectivity is a unique kind of apprehension. Fearing discloses something as threatening, but this is not a matter of first ascertaining a future evil and then fearing it. "Fearing ... has already disclosed the world, in that out of it something like the fearsome may come."[26] This differs from Dewey's view of emotionally charged sense in saying that in at least one basic family of cases perception and feeling are part of a single phenomenon.

Rorty rightly indicates the limitations of this reading of Dewey in characterizing his philosophy as "edifying rather than systematic."[27] It may instead be seen as ambiguous in its analysis of emotion as well as neutral between competing interests. These qualities would explain its attractiveness to a variety of theoretical viewpoints which are themselves normally opposed.[28] However they would also justify trying to differentiate between accounts which are not distinguished by Dewey and trying to show that his neutrality between interests does not extend to neutrality between competing conceptions of interests. The alternative account of emotion as distinctively affective or practical perception avoids the assumptions of his theory of valuation, assumptions which appear to reflect cultural forms more accurately than commonalities of human psychological and social nature.

Dewey's theoretical conceptions are pervasive in our culture. Kohlberg adopts them when he detaches emotional judgments from moral thinking and advances a conception of moral development which is narrowly cognitive, ascribing no role to passions. They are also nicely exemplified by recent discussions of Richard Brandt and Jerome Shaffer. In reviewing them it becomes clear how their relative disinterest in emotions has a natural affinity with the calculative rationality typical of standard moral theory.

Brandt constructs a theory of the good and the right on the foundation of conditioning theory. The basic proposition is that we value things in virtue of their association with things previously or "natively" valued: "experiences become pleasant (or unpleasant) as a result of contiguity with other experiences already pleasant."[29] This "learned pleasantness" can be probed in cognitive psychotherapy – the complex "process of confronting desires with relevant information, by repeatedly representing it, in an ideally vivid way, at appropriate times."[30] Desires prove themselves to be rational if they do not diminish or disappear as a result. It is the basic role which such effects have in the criticism of desire and action that makes the facts of psychology so important for ethics, and the ethical theory which arises is inevitably utilitarian.

On Brandt's view there are several types of irrational desires. One type is based upon false beliefs about the means to some end already wanted. Such a desire will be extinguished "if the person repeats to himself the fact that he will not achieve the goals involved in instituting the desire by doing a certain thing." Another type comes from "artificial desire-arousal in cultural transmission." A desire which results from familiarity with other persons' attitudes is typically irrational because it disappears if one repeatedly reminds oneself that social (i.e., external) standards have no necessary connection with our own desires. This fact wreaks havoc with emotional evaluations and essentially limits rational desires to those which are native and those which are rationally derived from native desires. These desires may include the interest in others' well being which we call "benevolence" – either because it is native or because it is conditioned so early as to be very resistant to extinction – but there is clearly no room for the rational compassion which depends upon a norm of suffering.[31] Since the authority of norms is undermined by critical questioning, rational desires must refer to perceived benefits rather than to justified emotions. In Brandt's account, the philosophical conclusions seem validly derived from his theoretical assumptions. But if the conclusions are dubious, so too is the psychological theory which entails them – a reminder of the easy acceptance in psychology of assumptions which have a largely philosophical basis. The assumptions of Hume's associationism are far from universal, of course. Brandt notes that "some psychologists" doubt that conditioning explains "our enjoyment of the plaudits of the multitudes, the discomfort of knowing that a person has a very negative reaction towards one, etc."[32] One obvious justification for such doubts is given by the sort of theory sketched by Rousseau. On his maturationist account of desire the most significant human motivations are neither merely native nor products of conditioning. They are justifiable when abstract "laws of nature" are given an appropriate interpretation. This is not the imposition of external standards but intelligent formulation of reasonable expectations.

Shaffer's views have equally extreme implications for the connection between reason and emotion. Assume with him that emotions are sets of physiological processes and sensations caused by certain beliefs and desires. If we regard these desires and beliefs in the following way, the emotions lose much of their interest. In a case of fear, an obstruction looms in the path and one changes direction, believing that some bodily harm is otherwise likely and desiring not be harmed. But, having separated out the components in this way, the emotion itself seems to become superfluous. We need not refer to it in explaining the behavior: the belief and the desire are sufficient to account for the action quite independently of the feelings they cause. Likewise, in assessing the emotion we need do no more than to assess the belief and the desire. "That a person's emotion is rational or irrational does not imply that his or her physiological responses pass or fail to pass the test but just that his or her beliefs and desires do."[33]

It is questionable, on this account, whether emotions have an essential or even a desirable place in our lives. They lose any motivational salience, since rational assessment of the desire-belief component of emotion is sufficient for decision. We should therefore give up James's notion that our passional nature must decide between options when intellect cannot, the physiological-sensational component being unable to yield decisions. Emotions also lose their evaluative relevance. A life of belief, desire, and action without emotion appears conceivable, and we can "imagine individual lives and even a whole world in which things would be much better if there were no emotion."[34] As long as the distinction of the desire-belief component from the feeling element is valid, a broadly negative assessment of the place of emotion in life is plausible.

Accounts which analyze emotions into elements of desire, belief, and feeling differ in ways we will examine further below. All of them are challenged, though, by phenomenological accounts which avoid the implausibilities of faculty psychology and define a rational role for affectivity. In maintaining that affectivity brings us into relationship with other beings, Heidegger describes emotion as a condition of the possibility of experience, not as one outcome of experience. His description of fear implies that we should be equally wary of the distinction between physiological responses on the one hand and desire and belief on the other and of the distinction between belief and desire itself.

There is a serious impediment for any conception which sticks to phenomenological insistence on pure description. It is one thing to criticize psychological theories for embedding dubious philosophical theories, but it is quite another to oppose scientific reflection on the psychological matters of interest to philosophers. Scheler adopts the second position in his determination to avoid any "reduction" of feeling to understanding and to prevent the "denial of intentional feeling and the abandonment of the entire emotional life to a descriptive psychology and its causal explanations."[35] Pressing the view that emotions are *sui generis,* he claims that they possess "their own original laws" and are "as independent of the psychophysical organization of man as pure thought."[36] But it is not a very convincing attack on analytical categories which itself insists upon a categorical distinction between matters of interest to philosophy and phenomena amenable to scientific explanation. There is no good reason to doubt that a satisfactory account of emotions will include contributions by empirical psychology. On the contrary, as we will shortly see, scientific evidence provides invaluable weapons against conceptions of emotion which Scheler wishes to reject. If the philosophical presuppositions of modern psychological theory can be avoided, it should be possible to regain a view of morality as rational without succumbing to an anti-scientific attitude of mind. To be avoided is only what McDowell describes as the "philistine scientism ...based on the misleading idea that the right of scientific method to rational acceptance is discernible from a more objective standpoint than that from which we seem to perceive ...saliences."[37]

II Practical perception

Heidegger speaks of "the specific ecstatical unity which makes it existentially possible to be afraid."[38] In order to retrieve the issue concerning us here from this difficult vocabulary, let us say that the sentence, "I believed that bodily harm was likely and I desired not to be harmed," is not a simple conjunction. Neither part of the claim can be understood in isolation from the other. "Harm" does not refer to an empirically describable state about which we might have beliefs without being appropriately motivated. Either the reference to harm includes an evaluation, so that the belief is logically related to the desire; or "harm" refers to an empirically describable state, in which case it does not adequately represent the cognitive aspect of the emotion. Fear is justified if the situation which evokes it is fearful, and no description is sufficient warrant for such an evaluation. Harm, therefore, should be understood appraisively, in which case the recognition of potential harm has motivational force. This is not to say that whenever we recognize harm we must desire security but that the capacity for such recognitions and the capacity for such desires are interdependent.[39] Practical perception involves both desire and judgment but not as separable elements. They are "internally related."

It is sometimes possible to explain actions in desire-belief terms which resemble a description of practical perception but lack the complex relationship of purpose and judgment typical of emotions. One may seek to avoid a collision, believing that it will cause broken bones and (perhaps for instrumental reasons) not wanting any broken bones. Unlike a case of fearful avoidance there is no judgment about impending harm here. That judgment includes a reason for action, whereas a judgment about broken bones becomes a reason only when conjoined with a desire. Practical or emotional perception, in contrast to the instrumentalist description of practical reasoning, is characterized by appraisive beliefs internally related to purposes.

An account of emotion as practical perception should distinguish itself from cognitivist theories of emotion which also give beliefs or judgments a central place. Cognitivism represents evaluative judgments as necessary conditions for emotions. This is a much stronger claim than the relationship between emotional evaluation and the good life described in chapter 2. A description of experience does not include necessary connections, there being no experiential difference between what is the case and what must be. The task of identifying necessary connections is that of theory. However no theory follows unambiguously from the psychological evidence, and in any event the cognitivist analysis of emotion is compromised by a great deal of conceptual and scientific evidence.

On a cognitivist view, shame is distinguished by a judgment of responsibility for some situation. While Lord Byron was not responsible for having a clubfoot, however, he is said to have been ashamed of it, so that his emotion lacks the judgment required by a cognitivist account.[40] By itself this is not decisive against the cognitivist, who might reply, following Marchand's *Byron*: "The boy early developed a sensitiveness to his lameness, perhaps because his mother upbraided him for it in her exasperated moods."[41] To upbraid is to blame, and to be sensitive to blame is to accept the responsibility required by the cognitivist account. This response, though, is unacceptable. Byron had to know that he was not at fault for a condition which he in no way produced, so that on the cognitivist explanation of his shame it entails a pair of blatantly contradictory judgments. Surely, though, it would be more plausible to account for the emotion as the result of associations between his mother's rebukes and misdeeds for which he was justifiably criticized. (It is this sort of faulty emotion that accounts like Brandt's handle well.) The once-bitten-twice-shy phenomenon can be treated in the same way. Having been attacked by a vicious dog, a person may become afraid of even obviously harmless ones. On the cognitivist account, the fearer of dogs inconsistently believes of some both that they are dangerous and that they are not. By supposing that the fear reflects an association established between the vicious animal and others canines, in contrast, the irrational judgment disappears.[42] Because we can understand the situations in this way our concepts of shame and fear do not require an evaluative judgment to occur in all instances of the emotions.

Neither example absolutely refutes the cognitivist case. Perhaps the precocious Byron believed in the doctrine of reincarnation and thought of himself as visited by the sins of a former life. Perhaps the lap dog appears friendly, but for all one really knows it may be rabid. These may not be reasonable beliefs but they are not absurd. Cognitivists can always accommodate difficult cases by embellishing a story until the required judgment gains a place without introducing blatant incoherence. However such defences are implausibly ad hoc when set against psychological facts showing that affective responses can occur without any prior cognitive discrimination.

Animals and infants exhibit fear which is best regarded as a reflex rather than the expression of a value judgment. Even in adult human beings emotions can be produced without an intervening evaluative judgment: drugs can induce emotional states independently of any information from external circumstances; and emotions can be produced by sensory inputs without involving the brain's neo-cortex, which presumably functions in evaluative judgments of the kind recognized by cognitivists.[43] There is abundant other evidence showing that emotional reactions often occur without prior cognitive acts.[44] Even this does not leave the cognitivist account completely defenseless. Simple affective states, it could be replied, are not emotions properly so called. However the dispute with anti-cognitivists then becomes a verbal one, and arbitrary remedies will not interest us for long.

The evidence undermines cognitivism in virtue of the theory's demand that judgments occur in all cases of emotion. The same evidence is consistent with the view of emotions as practical perception because that account does not claim that judgments accompany emotions in every case. The connection is normal but not logically necessary. Our appraisive judgments owe their meaning to the emotions they characterize in that without experience of the emotions we could not formulate the judgments. It is nonetheless possible for some instances of a emotion to occur without the characteristic judgment or for the judgment to occur dispassionately.

The case, put positively and in conformity with the scientific evidence, is that an emotion is a pattern of discriminative response. In order to identify a primitive or unlearned reaction as fear, it must be possible to recognize it as aversive. We can speak of this aversion as indicating the basic informational content of the emotion and regard it not as a covert judgment but as a condition of judgment. Fright and fear provide a simple model. Occurrences of the responses (whether environmentally or artificially evoked) which we call fright display the discriminatory capacity which in mature fear is represented by the concept of danger. Lacking the discriminatory capacity the concept would not be formed, but unlike this innate capacity the concept is learned. The fully-developed emotion depends upon a history of experience, familiarity with a family of cases which shapes a particular conception of danger and makes it possible to formulate judgments of danger in the absence of particular occurrences of the emotion.

Emotions include a place for judgments. We acknowledge this place in refusing to ascribe fear to persons who do not identify something as a threat or behave as if something is a threat. The full complexity of this relationship is clear, however, only when we recognize not only that fear includes a discriminative capacity but also that this capacity is essential for the concept of danger, so that the concept does not arise separately from fear. Danger is a bad thing. It is tied to the desire for security which is also typical of fear, and its "repulsiveness" thus results from the emotional state which is in turn defined by a proposition about danger. In consequence, danger is meaningless to one who cannot be afraid, so that even if we may upon occasion believe fearlessly that danger is present the judgment depends upon a structure of experience which includes fear.

If these reflections are right, emotional events occur prior to learning and without good evidence. Elementary experiences of fear, for example, are not bound by the standards of evidence which result when experience permits distinguishing between real and apparent harm and leads to a particular interpretation being placed upon the original discriminative response. Once such distinctions are made we are sensitive to standards of evidence which occasion judgments of validity and truth, but until that time aversive behavior expresses an untutored feeling associated with natural responses to real or apparent causes of fright. Fear is educated fright in which the informational structure of the latter has taken on a settled significance.

An important implication of the complexity of emotional experience is that, while it requires the rejection of cognitivism, it gives no support to the anti-cognitivist case that only feelings are necessary for an emotion to be the emotion it is. Like other attempts to identify some particular element as the principal mark of an emotion's identity, this affectivist view takes it for granted that emotions have some essential condition of this kind. Starting from this assumption and recalling the limitations of cognitivist accounts, it is deceptively easy to infer that feelings rather than judgments primarily identify emotions. Byron's inappropriate shame can be understood if his emotion was a matter of what he felt rather than what he believed, in which case feelings can determine the identity of an emotion independently of any accompanying cognition.[45]

We saw above how a cognitivist might avoid this conclusion, and arguments for the priority of feelings over judgments are generally inconclusive. One such argument asks us to imagine an anomalous emotion in which judgment conflicts with feeling.

There might be a case in which one makes the evaluative judgment which goes with grief – that something of great value has been irretrievably lost – while experiencing the feeling typical of having been narrowly saved from serious injury. To call this grief, as the judgment would suggest, would clearly be wrong. It would be equally wrong, however, to treat this as evidence of feelings overriding judgments in the identification of emotional states. The feeling in this case is relief, an intentional state attached to judgments of danger, and the emotional feeling and belief can not here be extricated. When feelings and beliefs are clearly distinct, the feelings no longer identify emotions. The judgment of loss might be accompanied by the feeling of being tickled, and again this would not be grief; but it would not be an instance of an emotion-determining feeling, since the co-occurrence of a judgment of loss and a bodily sensation does not constitute an emotional state. There is no good reason for supposing that feelings fare any better than judgments as candidates for the primary element in the identification of emotions.

An analogy with sense perception explains this a little more fully. Vision can occur in human beings in the absence of visual sensations. Persons with cerebral lesions sometimes accurately report the shapes and colors of objects before their eyes although they also report seeing nothing. Visual information is evidently being processed in the absence of its familiar sensory dimension. It is reasonable to suppose that visual sensations occur only in persons with intact visual systems and reasonable to entertain the possibility that in animals with more primitive nervous systems vision occurs without sensation.[46] In any event, "seeing something" has a clear sense in which seeing does not entail having sensations. For similar reasons, it is reasonable to suppose that the processing of emotional information – running "affect programs" as Paul Ekman describes it[47] – does not depend upon the occurrence of feelings. The fright response of birds and young mammals may well occur without feeling. However, fully developed affective perception requires a healthy and sophisticated nervous system, so that the capacity to feel is related to the capacity to learn from experience, to form conceptual judgments, and so on. Scientific reflection thus counts against the affectivist view as well as against the cognitivist account.

If emotions are thought of as clusters of feelings, judgments, and desires, and if neither feelings nor judgments are the essential ingredient in an emotion, then desires might fill this role. In contrast to dispassionate judgments guided by good evidence, emotional conceptions are often based on insufficient or poorly scrutinized grounds. In contrast to the generalizability of judgments, emotional reactions may display a decided particularity: behavior of a kind that annoys us in most people can be amusing in a person we love. These features of emotions reflect desires. The desires one has for a lover easily override normal judgment and make bad habits seem amusing. Again, being viscerally afraid of an animal is to have an intense desire to stay alive and unharmed, and this desire determines the view of the animal as a threat to these purposes. These desires work so strongly that they determine our emotional conceptions rather than those conceptions determining our desires. Hence, it can be suggested, we should look to desires in determining the identity of an emotion.[48]

It is not only the many cases in which judgments deflate emotional desires that compromise this analysis. More persuasive is the explanation that the desires for which the account is plausible have cognate judgments. The desire to remain unbitten does not make something appear fearsome unless it is also the desire to remain unharmed. In this event, to say that the desire for safety from harm determines the appearance of threat or danger mistakes an "internal" or "logical" relationship for an external or causal one.

Like the other proposed analyses, this account assumes that one or another of judgment, feeling, or desire is primary in emotions. Taken together, the arguments and evidence each amasses call the others into question and thereby cast doubt on the shared assumption. The concepts of judgment, feeling, and desire are useful for describing certain kinds of experience systematically, but it does not follow that any of them correspond to elemental features of emotion. On the contrary, when used as tools of analysis they seem to disguise important interrelationships, drawing too simple a sketch of a complex reality and making it difficult to see emotional perception as at once and indistinguishably evaluative and purposive.

The analytical treatment of emotion is limited in what it can accomplish because it gets no further than such determinations as: "judgment does not entail emotion." This cornerstone of anti-cognitivism is an unhelpful platitude or worse, since it may discourage due attention to the intimate connection between the capacity for emotional judgment and the capacity for emotional desire. It is a waste of time to seek a general answer to the question whether in emotion it is judgments which determine desires or desires which determine judgments, or whether it is feelings, judgments, or desires which constitute particular emotions. If there is such a thing as practical perception, it can be adequately described only through a holistic account in which none of these aspects of emotions is understood as distinct from the others.

Perhaps, though, in calling for such an account we promote a myth. McDowell's doubts about "perceptions of saliences" become skeptical objections in Williams's exploration of views of "the knowledge given by applying ethical concepts as something like perception."[49] Like other emotional concepts, these are "thick" concepts whose use is tied to social customs and circumstances and includes both description and evaluation of an object. The relevant test of the notion that such concepts can define perceivable moral qualities is the comparison to the perception of "secondary qualities" like colors.

The physical world may present itself as different colors to different kinds of observers, or as something other than a color to observers who are different in other ways. These qualities are representations of the world that is there independent of our experiences and perspectives. Ethical qualities are not entirely like this. The environment of human beings may evoke different appraisals in members of different traditions, and in still others it may evoke something other than an evaluative belief. But Williams can find no ethical analogy to the fact that reflection on color perception enables us to place our perceptions in relation to those of observers who are differently made and to see how these perceptions can give knowledge of physical reality. The ethical analogy would require going outside local judgments to a reflective account which both explains and justifies them. But while there might be social-scientific explanations of these local conceptions (for example, Marx's view of moral beliefs as reflections of economic circumstances), they would not also show that they reflect a correct view of moral reality. Through what process then, could "a range of investigators rationally, reasonably, and unconstrainedly come to converge on a determinate set of ethical conclusions"? Williams answers,

> If it is construed as convergence on a body of ethical truths which is brought about and explained by the fact that they are truths – this would be the strict analogy to scientific objectivity – then I see no hope for it. In particular, there is no hope of extending to this level the kind of world-guidedness we have been considering in the case of the thick ethical concepts.[50]

This argument indicates how important it is to recognize the place of emotions in the moral form of life. The thick, but abstract, concepts necessary for getting about in any social world are interpreted within particular ways of life in such a way that local conceptions include modes of discriminating between right and wrong beliefs. The psychology of the emotions exhibits general facts of human nature and universals of emotional judgment, and the possibility of gaining reasoned agreement lies in this. The identification of situations corresponding to various thick concepts is dependent upon social criteria, but because such normative criteria exist, moral judgments can be publicly assessed. Human nature in this respect provides an objective grounding for ethical life. Still missing, though, is any analogy to Williams's criterion for perception, namely a connection between the observations of one kind of observer and those of other kinds which would explain their judgments by reference to truths independent of particular social worlds. That would require not only that participants in any human way of life share a concept of the good but also that any social being whatever makes judgments which could be explained as representations of an independent social reality. Since social realities are constituted by their members, this requirement of independence seems to be incoherent.

Several possibilities for rescuing the notion of practical or affective perception exist at this juncture. Following Rorty, we could argue that we do not have any idea of what it would be like to account for the world in absolute terms. This says, in effect, that Williams's criterion for perception is too strong, depending upon an unintelligible condition. Or, following Taylor, we could argue that the subject-related descriptions characteristic of the human sciences lie outside the absolute account of reality which is the appropriate ideal of the natural sciences. This implies that affective awareness is distinguished from sensory perception by including the interpretive dimension in which inherent disputability works against convergence. On this view we should expect significant disanalogies between sensory and affective perception, but they do not compromise the philosophical usefulness of either concept.[51] Finally, we could maintain that to appreciate the fact of psychological universals is to recognize that patterns of discriminatory response, sensory or affective, make possible the kind of explanatory account Williams demands. Moral judgments can be traced to representations of reality in a way consistent with the interpretations central to the social construction of the moral world.

Rorty's proposal suggests that, while moral realities are not external to human lives in the way that physical reality is thought to be external to perceivers, the distinction does not support the intuition that physical reality is somehow more real. The thought might be supported by arguing that our primary encounters with the world are broadly emotional, scientific conceptions of physical reality which abstract from the meaning of events for subjects being secondary and derivative. By taking the derivative case as the standard one and identifying the abstraction with "objective reality" or with the "world as it exists," the concept of evaluation is misrepresented and the affective cognition characteristic of ordinary thinking is overlooked. Where to take the point from here is unclear, however, and Taylor's argument appears to offer greater opportunity for constructive explorations of moral judgment. It helps to show emotional judgments as subject to rational examination, reflection, correction, in short to place them near perception in any standard contrast between perception and feeling. Unfortunately, it does not resolve the difficult problem of discriminating the notion of practical perception from views which pull emotional judgment towards the feeling end of such a spectrum. Even a champion of the education of emotions like Diamond fudges differences in explicating her conception of thinking about moral matters by saying in Deweyan fashion that "thinking well involves thinking charged with appropriate feeling."[52] In apparent contrast to Nussbaum's otherwise similar conception of moral judgments as expressing perceptions of moral realities, this view resembles the Humean doctrine that there is no such access to interesting moral knowledge.

Williams, Baier, Diamond, Lovibond, and Nussbaum agree in seeing moral judgments as expressions of emotion and emotions as central in the psychology of the moral life. They also agree in denying any sharp contrast between emotion and reason and in questioning the rationalist philosophy whose moral psychology emphasizes a supposed dichotomy between reason and emotion. Their accounts of emotion differ, however, in the details of their characterization of the relationship between emotion and reason. In understanding emotional judgment as lacking anything like a representative quality, Williams and Baier are close to Hume and Dewey. On their accounts, moral sentiments can be corrected and made long-sighted and concerned with system, harmony, and consistency. They gain this validity as a result of social interaction. In order to adopt the moral point of view, to be a moral judge, one has to be willing to make the mutual adjustments needed for a stable point of view to be possible; and the virtues found in moral judges are abilities to function in company with others. In short, emotions respond to recognized canons of social reasonableness. As Baier remarks, the correction of sentiments "can be done by sentiment and custom, and is not the prerogative of a purely intellectual 'reason.'"[53]

To speak of affective perception is equally to dismiss "a purely intellectual 'reason,'" so that this alone is not distinctive of the Humean view. Nor is stress upon the role of public discourse in the correction and interpretation of emotional judgments. The distinction comes down to the perceived intimacy of relationships between judgment, desire, and feeling. On the Hume-Dewey view, the function of reason is secretarial, organizing schedules of desires, finding reasonable accommodations, etc. Desire, though, is the boss, and reason must ultimately accept its decrees. This view is a fairly modest reform of the orthodox prescriptive account of moral judgment. The view of emotion as perception is more radical, denying the line of authority defined by the Hume-Dewey account and locating judgment in the inner office.

For many purposes of moral inquiry, including matters of moral education, it may not be very important how, or if, this matter is decided. The competing views both blunt the contrast between reason and emotion and ally themselves against the narrow view of moral philosophy whose distinctive practical expression is elaborated in the next chapter. To this extent, it is not necessary to worry problems on the frontier between philosophy and psychology. Insofar as moral education is to be viewed as including the education of emotions, however, the above differences have matching practical implications. If the role of reason is secretarial, education will properly fall under the paradigm of scheduling and accommodation; if it has an executive role, the appropriate paradigm will be skill and sensitivity in interpretation. On the one hand, moral education is learning to cope with a vast variety of feelings and situations; on the other hand, it is learning how to see.

It is in helping to decide between these alternatives that the third response to Williams's argument must prove itself. Its strength is the opportunity it provides to state a naturalistic view of emotional and moral judgment along the lines of sensory judgments. There is no fundamental difficulty in placing emotional perceptions of danger, novelty, suffering, and excellence in relation to the perceptions of other people and other creatures, since the psychological capacities underlying perception of these qualities and such secondary qualities as colors alike have evolved so that the world will present itself to us in reliable and useful ways. The social explanation of divergent local judgments occurs on top of this psychological explanation, which fulfills "the project of giving to ethical life an objective and determinate grounding in considerations about human nature." Williams regards this project as "comprehensible" but "not ... very likely to succeed."[54] The prospects brighten only when we have available an account of the emotional origin of moral concepts which ties them to basic desires. The view of emotion as practical perception provides this.

It does not, at least so far, completely explain how to reconcile the objectivity of moral judgment with its tendency to divergence. Where interpretation flourishes, conceptions of the good compete. The psychological explanation of sensory perception justifies perceptual judgments by showing how they give knowledge of physical reality; the psychological explanation of emotional perception leaves the question of knowledge partly open because it does not show how competing views of the good can be harmonized or why they should be. It is notable that, there being no grounds for universalizing the judgments typical of emotions, it is possible to value the morality of one's own society as distinctive or discriminatory. The objectivity of emotional claims thus differs from that of descriptive utterances which are universalizable in the sense that the same claim can be made of anything similar in all perceivable respects. That

moral qualities owe their identity in part to interpretive understandings places a continuing strain on the perceptual analogy.

III *Improving our emotional vision*

To experience familiar human sentiments and to exercise the
human senses are alike to perceive the world in characteristic
ways. Some ideas typical of a conservative epistemology are
useful in relieving the strains we have seen to plague this comparison. Echoing Burke and Scheler, Hans-Georg Gadamer
stresses the importance of pre-established expectations, or prejudices, in understanding moral rationality. Trying "to restore to
its rightful place a positive concept of prejudice that was driven
out of our linguistic usage by the French and English Enlight-
enment," he maintains that "prejudices, in the literal sense of the
word, constitute the initial directedness of our whole ability to
experience."[55] Only such presuppositions enable us to assimilate
information, deal with novelty, and gain knowledge. Unlike accounts of knowledge which assume that issues can be settled by
reference to a neutral standard, the conservative perspective regards all claims as subject to reinterpretations of this background.

The notion that reasoning is possible only against a set of
background understandings is as true of Lovibond's Wittgenstein as of Gadamer. In order to think at all or to make sense of
the world we inhabit, we must, she says, "maintain a posture of
uncritical acceptance towards a certain core of intellectually authoritative institutions."[56] Knowledge cannot be severed from
the community of expectations or the historicity of our existence.
Nor, it can be added to this view which "sounds like pragmatism,"[57] can knowledge be severed from features of human development. To the prejudices of history can be added those natural to sensation and emotion. If innate patterns of discriminatory response are parts of our information-processing mechanism, they constitute fixed points for our humanity in addition

to our historical horizons. Since these discriminatory mechanisms are too simple to constitute judgments they cannot themselves be prejudices, but they support prejudices of the species, including those abstract agreements defining the concept of the good.

It is obviously necessary to extend these epistemological notions beyond nature and history. These two sets of prejudices enable conflicts to occur which no appeal to sentiment or tradition can resolve. Especially where traditions are weak, the differing interpretations of the good to which abstract emotional agreements are inherently subject divide and isolate individuals and communities. The absence of a dependable historical standard against which to assess these disagreements is a philosophically powerful incentive to produce a timeless one, as has been expressed through recourse to a narrow or two-level account of morality which identifies rational principles capable of isolating disagreements within the arena of personal preferences. Part of the strength of the conservative position is the weakness of this alternative, appeal to metaphysical notions of our common humanity yielding no universally rational principles. The limitation of the position is that universal social and psychological similarities lack any immediate normative implications. Cultural roots and native emotional capacities impose no a priori norms of behavior.

To a small extent this limitation is softened by the possibility of providing an historical explanation of universal principles. The course of social evolution for some cultures in which differences of moral interpretation became common includes the development of political rights and principles which protect all particular viewpoints, enforcing a modus vivendi. Seen from this perspective, classical liberalism defends a form of human association which guarantees a private sphere in which any possible vision of the good can be embraced unencumbered by moral knowledge. The principle that the state remains neutral toward controversial ideals of the good life may be highly valued, but it does not, from this perspective, appear to have any independent foundation. That is, the existence of universal political rights is not understood as justifying liberal society in virtue of their permanent validity but as constituting such a society and determining its modes of self-understanding. Such rights are themselves expressions of one possible conception of the good, namely that it is good for individuals to define for themselves what is good.

As a reflection of the philosophically powerful incentive to produce a timeless standard for assessing disagreements, this liberal view is a clear failure. If it replaces the attempt to provide a theory of the good with a non-partisan moral theory, the latter theory remains controversial. It gives no way of addressing anti-liberal attitudes which conflict with the liberal aspiration for self-definition of the good. It is, by contrast, a second strength of the conservative conception that it includes resources for addressing this problem. The constraints of nature and history are further softened by the fact that nothing in this conception limits the horizons of moral understanding to the past. While the reflective and argumentative processes of special interest to philosophy generate divergent understandings, they also include possible practices which enable traditions and interpretations to converge. Prejudices can be corrected by argument which addresses oppositions between conceptions of the good as long as this argument is not represented on the model of deductive inference from rational principles characteristic of modern moral theory. More promising forms can be found in conceptions of rhetoric, conversation, dialogue, and literary encounter.

In order to seek the processes of moral convergence and consensus rather than the compromise of modus vivendi, we might look to Aristotle's account of discussions among the many, except that his account of political deliberation did not take moral differences very seriously, or even recognize them, being subject to the ideological distortions of his doctrine of natural superiors. In order to honor differences appropriately, we might instead look to Freire's *Pedagogy of the Oppressed*. Describing "dialogical" education involving "revolutionary leaders," Freire says that the teachers from outside aim not to give information but to engage in "thematic investigation" of the "ideas, values, concepts, and hopes" of their students, leading to a "synthesis" of the world views of both parties to the enrichment of both. Because the investigation involves such a synthesis, it does not simply serve the aspirations of one party. It does not bind the teachers passively to an alien vision, and it does not constitute a cultural invasion. It constitutes a mode of reaching consensus through communication.[58]

Later we will also look at Habermas's model of discussion leading to the formation of "generalizable interests." Rather than focusing on single, reflecting agents, Habermas gives primacy of place to the community of persons in discussion. Only through the processes of discursive will-formation in which proposed values are submitted for examination by all others can we determine whether an interest is generalizable or capable of rational consensus. This "dialogical" pursuit of valid common purposes contrasts strongly with the "monological" discussions conducted by modern philosophers' moral agents and promoted by the moral educators we become acquainted with below. It promises to lead to valid purposes of the kind deemed impossible by the epistemology which denies knowledge of the good.

These are complex and problematical ideas. They conceal important differences. Habermas is certainly not a moral conservative but a radical reformer who takes social structures seriously in a way that concentration on the participant's perspective cannot, and he does not share the anti-theoretical attitudes of most moral conservatives. While he views communication as crucial to forming social goods and values and identifies a number of presuppositions inherent in such communication, his presuppositions are neither biological constraints nor conventional prejudices but logical conditions for communication. As such they are markedly similar to the rational principles of modern moral theory, and they face many of the same problems. These problems are considered in chapter 5. At the same time we will explore possibilities for developing a model for the above metaphors – fusion, synthesis, generalization – capable of accommodating the diverse perspectives they reflect and showing what is right and what is wrong in the idea that "tradition is the best basis for the practical life."[59]

Our model should dispense with any philosophical conception of human nature. Given such a starting point we could determine "whether modern assumptions may be basically inhuman," but it is impossible to imagine arguments which would "determine the truth about these ultimate matters."[60] It is because philosophical discourse is in this sense characteristically "abnormal" that any useful conception of human nature will be more psychological than metaphysical. Only such a conception holds any promise of avoiding the skeptical extremes of pure philosophy, making it reasonable to explore what processes of reaching a consensus in modern society might be like and vindicating MacIntyre's "Aristotelian" rejection of the modern "thesis that questions about the good life for man or the ends of human life are to be regarded from the public standpoint as systematically unsettlable."[61]

This model is consistent with the conservative emphasis on the passions, enabling us to treat disagreements about evaluation as differences in interpretation of the same basic human purposes and to imagine conversations overcoming the barriers to agreement built into moral ways of life. The prejudices of curiosity, pride, and resentment consist in distinctive ideas, and these ideas have a practically limited range of possible interpretations. The corresponding purposes have the support of good reasons when the prejudices are educated by experience and argument. Underlying such rational desires is a kingdom of human ends described by Rousseau rather than Kant, a system of shared meanings and agreements about the kinds of things which can be intelligently desired. While these underlying meanings are abstract rather than those of a particular community, their existence entails that any two moral traditions should be "able to recognize each other as advancing moral contentions on issues of importance" and confirms MacIntyre's further reflection that all human traditions "share some common features."[62] Thus any two can in principle be part of the same interpretive circle.

The important fact is that natural agreements do exist. A fully articulated moral conservatism would include a precise statement of their relationship to culturally specific expressions of emotion, so as to define the limits of agreement; but here it is enough to recognize that without these agreements no moral community would be possible. Given them we all possess a common concept of the good life shaped by desirable ends. We may construe these ends differently, but their existence lets us envisage the creation of common points of view even within pluralistic civilization. We know how to compare diverse conceptions of novelty, achievement, injury, etc., and we are able to understand the associated purposes in the light of the rational expectations which give these ends a concrete form different from our own. During this imaginative sharing of alternative bodies of experience and tradition our perspectives may expand and we come to understand what was unclear.

Adults and children, champions and novices, friends and strangers assess novelty, achievement, and injury differently; but this is not a barrier to mutual understanding. The same is true of differences between traditions and ways of life: they are differences of the same logical kind, for the concept of the good for human beings provides a key of interpretation. It opens another door as well. Discourse about the practical life does not have to be backward-looking. The future is also a relevant horizon, and we can formulate expectations as to what that future should be. While this process may begin from existing traditions, it is not bound by them. "We are limited in how we can start if not in where we may end up."[63] We can certainly set out to change conventions and the rights attaching to them.

While the meanings we share are local they are not embodied solely in social traditions, for they are also changed during the discussions which enable people to agree in their characterizations of behavior and reach a consensus on the good. These possibilities are generally ignored or summarily denied by current movements in moral education. These schools tend to eschew exploration of the conditions of "synthesis" in matters of value and have little to say about the capacity of "dialogical" (as opposed to clarifying) discussion to promote convergence in appraisals. Little but not nothing. In his latest work Kohlberg has asserted that the best developed "reasoning procedure logically requires dialogue in actual real-life moral conflicts."[64] This claim is extravagant, but its more important limitations are not evident until it is clear why he considers the role of discussion only in the development of principles of moral reasoning, ignoring its contribution to agreements which are achievable within communities. To sort this out requires a closer look at his educational views and others like them.

By showing systematically that the emotions may be viewed as primary factors in human well-being and that an account of emotions needs to attend to the rational aspects of evaluation, the scope of moral education is extended to serious inquiry into meaningful purposes. By seeing that such purposes define a common concept of the good life, the philosophical assumptions of prevalent educational practices are thrown into relief which makes those practices stand in need of a different justification. Consideration of two cases which stress chosen rather than rational desires conclusively demonstrates this need.

Chapter 4

Education for Choice

I Values Clarification.

Moral education includes the passing on of complex patterns of approval and disapproval from one generation to the next. In so doing it forms character, developing persons with appropriate virtues and sensitivity to customary relationships and their obligations. In this way it exercises an indirect influence on conduct, but it is not specifically concerned with determining what to do in problematic situations which call for good judgment rather than accurate calculation. It is thus learning how to see emotionally rather than to reason coldly. It occurs in schools and other formal institutions but mainly within families and other intimate spheres of association. There is more to it than this. It also involves the lessons of political relationships, and it may involve acquiring habits of reflection which compete with the needs of conformity. But it is at least these things.

Most of these claims are rejected by the main contemporary schools of moral education, which share conceptual foundations in the modern conception of moral philosophy as normative theory. In spite of repeated assertions to the contrary, their points of mutual opposition are less important than this common foundation and the doctrines it supports. Many of the details are starkly apparent in Values Clarification. This school continues to draw heavy criticism for theoretical unclarity and shallowness, but the complaints are often unwarranted. Its doctrines well articulate many doubts and ideas pervasive in our culture, and they are often identical with those of more scholarly reputable proposals, including Kohlberg's cognitive-developmental approach.

The founders of Values Clarification claim with some plausibility to borrow their philosophy from John Dewey,[1] and they certainly share his aggressive and unapologetic pragmatism. They reject the view that there are fixed or final goods and subscribe, in Dewey's words, "to a belief in a plurality of changing, moving, individualized goods and ends, and to a belief that principles, criteria, laws are intellectual instruments for analyzing individual or unique situations."[2] In a free society, they teach, everyone is entitled to whatever values one may have, for values define "an area that isn't a matter of proof or consensus." Because desires and preferences are personal, it is inappropriate to tell a person, "You shouldn't like that" or "You shouldn't be interested in things like that." Likes and interests grow out of people's experience and are consistent with their lives, so that such admonitions "are in effect asking them to be hypocrites. We seem to be saying ... 'Yes, this is what your life has taught you, but you shouldn't say so. You should pretend that you had a different life.'"[3]

Values Clarification inveighs against the idea that "children are not people" but receptacles for adult beliefs. It rejects the "assumption ... that one does not have to practice valuing for oneself at an early age and that after twenty years or so of indoctrination one can readily break the habit of conforming to the values of others."[4] However it also recognizes that children are not simply tiny adults. Our ability to define goals for ourselves is not innate but has to be developed. This mastery is not likely to be spontaneous when the likes and interests which are consistent with one's life derive from competing attractions and form a system of ends which is itself inconsistent. Some kind of adult help is needed if one is to learn how to deal with the conflicts of desire which hinder growth of a coherent personality. If this help cannot legitimately take the form of designing a set of interests for individuals, it seems clear what form the assistance must take. Children should be engaged in situations which may evoke a value-clarifying response and enable them to sort matters out for themselves.[5]

These ideas oppose the Aristotelian notion of habituation to virtue, hence the idea that values education might centrally include precept and example, emotional appeals, or authoritative distinctions between desirable and undesirable behavior. In drawing the practical implications of a philosophical viewpoint in this way the Values Clarificationists reason justly, but difficulties arise when they also appear to move from practice to justification of those philosophical preferences. They hold that traditional methods have not and cannot lead to values in the sense that we are concerned with them, values that represent the free and thoughtful choice of intelligent humans interacting with complex and changing environments.

> In fact, those methods do not seem to have resulted in deep commitments of any sort. The values that are supposedly being promoted by those methods in our society – honor, courage, devotion, self-control, craftsmanship, thrift, love, and so on – seem less than ever to be the values that guide the behavior of citizens. On the pragmatic test of effectiveness alone, the approaches listed above must receive a low grade. They just do not seem to work very well....[6]

This statement is puzzling for its apparent acceptance of individuals uninterested in honor, self-control, or love; but it is fully comprehensible when we see that these words for virtues are understood semantically as praise-labels which only promote wishy-washiness – the analysis which runs from Hartshorne and May to Kohlberg.[7] The claim about traditional methods is also surprising for its concluding remark, which is belied by the "good behavior" often resulting from non-liberal forms of education. The discipline of Soviet classrooms, for example, is consistent with attentiveness, industry, devotion to society, and other accepted virtues, as well as with habits of criticism rather than simple acceptance of authority.[8] But the supposed impotence of traditional methods is wrongly understood as an empirical report about modern societies. It, too, is not counter-factual but semantical, following from a definition of "value."

For the Values Clarification theorists, no goal counts as a value unless it is (1) freely chosen (2) from a number of alternatives (3) after thoughtful consideration of the consequences of each alternative; unless (4) one prizes the choice and (5) is willing to affirm it publicly; and unless (6) one acts upon the choice (7) in repeated situations.[9] Values are thus defined in such a way that nothing inculcated or perceived deserves the name. However successful attempts to shape our preferences may be, they can never lead us to values as so defined unless all seven criteria are met.

Only by understanding these seven assertions as conceptual ones can we avoid the judgment that the claims of Values Clarification are false. At the same time we obviate other otherwise difficult questions. The conceptual elucidation of a concept does not require an inflexible list of defining criteria. We need not puzzle over how many sets of alternatives must be considered before a decision counts as expressing a genuine value, how long or thorough the deliberations must be, or whether one lacks values when circumstances make action and public affirmation dangerous.[10] Nor is it necessary to say that of two persons with identical conceptions of the good, one, having chosen a plan of life deliberately, has a mature set of values while the other, having been gently guided to identical objectives, has none. It is enough to note that the second of them falls short of a reflective ideal.

The Values Clarification account accurately reflects several aspects of our concept of value: that interests, goals, and ideals include a tendency to act on them; that over a large range of endeavor any thoughtful decision constitutes a correct choice for the person who makes it; that the things we prize belong to our view of the good. By expressing the concept in a less adamant way than its primary authors, values are depicted as purposes which human beings might actually have. In short, rather than regarding the seven criteria as essential conditions of having a value they can be regarded as an associated cluster of ideas. That the originators of the movement doggedly resisted any such revision is further evidence that the issue was linguistic rather than substantive.

The language misleadingly suggests that values are peculiar objects which one can become clear about but which are not affected by the process of clarification.[11] The emphasis upon deliberation about consequences, however, carries the implication that some purposes survive examination while others do not. It further implies that when alternatives multiply as a result of growing knowledge and experience our objectives change. A person "who has an important change in awareness or in patterns of experience might be expected to modify his or her values .... [V]alues evolve and mature as experiences evolve and mature." It therefore seems legitimate to "see values as being constantly related to the experiences that shape them and test them .... [T]hey are the results of hammering out a style of life .... [A]fter a certain amount of hammering ... [c]ertain things are treated as right, desirable, or worthy. These become our values."[12] In its logic, if not always in its articulation, the focus of Values Clarification is on the "changing, moving, individualized goods and ends" which define Dewey's philosophy of value.

Against this conceptual background the practices comprising Values Clarification often make good sense.[13] Like Socrates's intellectual "midwifery," the clarifying method consists largely in asking provocative questions, expressing approval of the answer, but pursuing one or two difficulties which the response might raise. In this way Socrates aimed at life according to virtue, whereas Values Clarification has no place for this behavioral concept; but the two approaches agree in seeking to shape clear understandings through a dialectic of question and answer. Comparison might also be made with Freire's notion of dialogical education and with the stress placed upon discussion in the latest versions of Kohlberg's view of development. We will return to these similarities later. The objectives of discussion for Socrates and Freire, in particular, test the assumption that values defy proof or consensus. The similarity of method conceals crucial disagreements about conceptions of value, desirable purposes, and appraisals of behavior.

The practices of Values Clarification rest on psychological assumptions claimed from Dewey. In many ways, Dewey's views are insightful and compelling, particularly his emphasis upon meanings and his elaboration of them as felt ideas. But Dewey's vision of maturity outruns his theory, which, in having no clear place for rational desires, precludes the consensus on the good sought by pre-modern philosophers. The same is true of the Values Clarificationists, although passages in which Dewey rejects "empirical theories" define potential pitfalls for their theory. Thus: "[t]he objection is that the theory in question holds down value to objects *antecedently* enjoyed, apart from reference to the method by which they come into existence; it takes enjoyments which are casual because unregulated by intelligent operations to be values in and of themselves."[14] Again: "[t]he fact that something is desired only raises the *question* of its desirability; it does not settle it."[15] But these points do not impinge upon the Values Clarification definition of value, which is consistent with Dewey's last word:

> Values (to sum up) may be connected inherently with liking, and yet not with *every* liking but only with those that judgment has approved, after examination of the relation upon which the object liked depends. A casual liking is one that happens without knowledge of how it occurs nor to what effect. The difference between it and one which is sought because of a judgment that it is worth having and is to be striven for, makes just the difference between enjoyments which are accidental and enjoyments that have value and hence a claim upon our attitude and conduct.[16]

It is easy to take the relationship between Dewey and Values Clarification too seriously, for both are "edifying rather than systematic." Let us then treat the connection as of primarily heuristic value and note that Values Clarification consistently supports an implicitly experimental method in which individuals formulate a system of purposes which are reasonable in the instrumentalist sense of incorporating acquired knowledge about what can be efficiently attained. It seems an easy inference that anyone who lacks a coherent plan of life will be subject to a variety of personality problems – apathy, flightiness, uncertainty, inconsistency, drifting, over-conformity, undue dissent, and excessive role-playing.[17] Apathy, uncertainty, and inconsistency are plausibly explained as effects of merely casual, hence often conflicting and easily frustrated likings. Conformity may be encouraged by lack of reasonable interests of one's own; and role-playing may result from seizing upon the example of others in the absence of any valuable interests. Or dissent may arise from having to get one's identity by opposing others when one has not achieved any personal identification of aims and interests. In general, such connections support the idea that individual well being can only be enhanced by achieving the clarity sought through the methods of Values Clarification.

Value development, whose criterion is value clarity, should on this view be measurable against such undesirable patterns of behavior; and those patterns can be expected to break down through effective use of clarifying techniques.[18] However the connection between Values Clarification exercises and action is never explicitly established,[19] so that apparent connections between clarity about values and patterns of behavior are not really explained. They can be taken to express the relationship between interests and action which characterizes practical reasoning, but because only the technical dimension of practical reasoning is considered the understanding of these interests is truncated. One result is a peculiar account of emotional needs and behavior which eventually leads to fatal problems.

Since needs are necessities, they are not like the objectives which are freely chosen from among sets of alternatives. For a time, advocates of Values Clarification explained this property of ends which are not "chosen desires" as a symptom of unmet emotional requirements. Such needs simply assail us and find expression in aggressiveness, withdrawnness, submissiveness, and signs of psychosomatic disorder – problems which must be resolved before the development of personal values can begin.[20] The describable contrast between behavior which is characteristic of confusion about values and of unmet needs is elusive,[21] but the distinction was deemed to define a type of personal problem for which the techniques of Values Clarification were not appropriate. The preconditions of free choice must be established before there can be reflective inquiry.

The idea that needs must be met before values can flourish provides a solid defense against seemingly decisive objections to Values Clarification as a form of moral education. Values Clarification ostensibly condones immorality. If one's values rest upon free choice from an unlimited number of alternative ways of life, then one might well choose a life of crime.[22] This option is not readily available, however, if values presuppose the prior satisfaction of certain needs, for these needs include "belonging" and being loved. Given such desires, no one could deliberately choose the life of a pariah, even if some, like Dickens's Artful Dodger, drift unawares into a criminal milieu. It is true that no moral or logical barrier exists to the choice of theft and other undesirable ways of life, but Values Clarification can recognize psychological obstacles to such choices. The existence of these obstacles justifies its optimism about humanity. Suggestions that Values Clarification encourages libertinism are unfounded because it has available a defense which is standard in contemporary accounts of evaluation. As R.M. Hare has insisted in response to similar charges, acceptable choice depends "upon the fortunate contingent fact that people who would take this logically possible view ... are extremely rare."[23] The version of this defense appropriate for Values Clarification is that the role of needs in the processes of human maturation establishes desirable psychological limits on the scope of individual choice.

These limits are not claims of reason. If they were, then the fact that values presuppose needs would permit the extension of clarifying techniques to those needs. This possibility could not be acknowledged, for it supports an account of value judgments which is inconsistent with the priority assigned to autonomous choice and action. If emotions were tied to judgments, the needs corresponding to them would be as liable to confusion as any other state of belief, hence as suitable subjects for clarification. We would be uncertain about what we needed – security or knowledge, say – until we were clear whether we felt anxiety or curiosity and whether the object of awareness was a danger apprehended or a novelty perceived. But rather than striving to increase one's ability to make such discriminations – and thereby acknowledging that some desires are amenable to proof or consensus – Values Clarification limits exploration of "affective domains" to "clarifying feelings – especially feelings of prizing and cherishing." These feelings are regarded as just "positive tones," not judgments.[24] As for emotions in particular, they conform to Abraham Maslow's view of "need-satisfactions that seem to be ends in themselves and not in need of any further justification or demonstration."[25] On this view, each individual has a number of "instinctoid" ends which are beyond justification, so that a person's well–being depends not upon conformity to rational standards but simply in certain satisfactions.

The "instinctoid" or "animal-like" conception of needs permits distinguishing them from wants in a way which does not concede a rational dimension to values. To construe needs as defining insistent ends-in-themselves is simply to understand them as wants or values of a special kind – ones to which there are no possible alternatives and ones which, in consequence, admit of no confusion. The need for security, for example, is an affective condition for having any set of reasonable interests. We want security if we want anything because without it no critically formulated desires and interests can occur. Other needs, such as the need for companionship, are also compulsions and differ from values only in virtue of their making certain choices feasible rather than themselves being freely chosen. The distinction between needs and values on this view is one between the wants which any human being has and those which, in incorporating the results of personal inquiry and experience, distinguish different individuals.

Pressing the account of needs this far goes beyond the explicit doctrines of Values Clarification. The leaders of the movement ultimately move in the opposite direction, dropping all discussion of emotional needs. The best explanation may be a tacit recognition that their behavioral distinctions between unmet needs and unclear values – aggression and overdissention, withdrawal and apathy, submission and overconformity, etc. cannot be sustained. The alternative mode of differentiating needs and values distinguishes rational from reasonable purposes, and because admitting rational purposes conflicts with the assumption that values are personal needs have to be removed from the account. This amendment is serious, since pruning off the account of needs removes the defense against charges of amorality. Still more serious is the failure to examine the surviving behavioral characterizations. Doing so reveals that the very formulation of Values Clarification includes a view of values as subject to tests of validity. The problem arises clearly out of a fundamental incoherence in the intuitive psychology on which Values Clarification is based.

In the light of supposed relationships between behavioral traits and the processes of valuing, the Values-Clarification account includes many claims which appear to be scientifically significant. Chief among them is the view that value-clarifying techniques lead to altered traits of behavior by creating a consistent system of motivations which mutually reinforce rather than conflict with one another. Few data bear out this claim. Empirical studies have shown that the initial enthusiasm with which value-clarifying activities are greeted by students quickly wanes and that no permanent behavioral improvements can be attributed to those processes. Nor is there any demonstrated impact on students' values or self-concepts.[26] These results contradict the predictions of the theory. They are exactly what one would expect if Values Clarification is simply an institutionalized expression of the uncertainty about values which it attempts to remedy.

There is a more basic explanation of the inability of Values Clarification to effect lasting behavioral changes. In one respect the process of maturation which is described in terms of filtering and channeling impulses through a screen of successful and unsuccessful strategies is not a clarifying process at all. Thoughts are subject to clarification but animal-like impulses are not. We may formulate clear means to ends and thereby generate coherent sets of desires from conflicting primitive urgings, but the impulses from which these reasonable desires derive remain incomprehensible. If we ask the reasons for them none can be forthcoming, so that the whole edifice of resulting values has a logically arbitrary foundation. Values lack ultimate reasons, and we might anticipate that persons who accept the ideal of rational inquiry are as likely to sink into a kind of apathy as to affirm and act upon desires which have no possible justification. In the absence of basic reasons for values, clarity about value could understandably lead to utter lack of certainty, to drifting among equally absurd alternatives and to dissent from meaningless purposes. Another alternative would be an existentialist leap into a preposterous faith. There are fundamental problems with a view whose plausible predictions can be so easily confounded by equally plausible contrary intuitions about behavior and whose optimism about reasonable people could be dashed by willingness to make irrational commitments. Yeats may have summed up these problems in the lines of his "Second Coming" following those quoted in the Introduction:

The ceremony of innocence is drowned;
The best lack all conviction, while the worst
Are full of passionate intensity.

The perception that values lack rational grounds is, in some periods, a familiar and dramatic feature of adolescence. It is no solution to this "crisis" to observe that we do have reasons for many desires. Any collection of ends is supported by the technical reflections which guide choice and by the coherence among chosen objectives which makes them mutually reinforcing. But rational agents seek the intrinsic reasons which give inherent meaningfulness to activity – the rational ends which imbue the other things we desire with significance. At least one source of such reasons, we have noted, is the emotions. The purposes characteristic of them are neither derived from other ends via a chain of means nor constituted by featureless impulses. During adolescence emotional impulses can easily appear groundless because of one's poor integration with the ways of social life which provide provisional norms of validity. The importance of this integration cannot be fully recognized as long as emotions are regarded as "positive tones" and "animal-like" feelings. Nor can the needed connections be established through modes of clarification which leave a person isolated in a set of merely personal values. They come about only through testing and choosing which are guided by argumentative discussion with others, but because such discussion aims at correct as well as clear conclusions it presupposes valid standards of evaluation of a kind which Values Clarification cannot fully endorse.

These dilemmas are most clearly present in the attempt to establish behavioral criteria for clarity and emotional well-being. The operative expressions – "apathetic," "aggressive," "over-conforming," "submissive," and the like – are semantically similar to words for virtues. They are "thick" concepts, evaluating behavior as well as describing it. This means that they either constitute "blame labels" and express personal assessments of behavior as undesirable, or they are used according to generally acknowledged standards of judgment. In the one case, no objective determination of clarity is possible and values education is pointless. In the other case, it is assumed that authoritative standards of evaluation exist, in which case clarity is an inadequate educational goal. Hence Values Clarification is either an incoherent practice or it unwittingly presupposes conditions for evaluation which entail that its aims are unduly modest.

If we can use words like "aggressive" and "apathetic" as behavioral characterizations, then we can do so with "courage," "honesty," and their opposites. If, in commanding expressions of the former kind, we are able to identify clarity about values, then in mastering logically similar expressions for virtues and vices we should be able to discriminate morally desirable and undesirable behavior as well. The very formulation of Values Clarification rests upon concepts whose standards of application can be agreed upon, and the very possibility of engaging in clarifying inquiry should lead us to see that agreements in both behavioral and moral characterizations do exist.

No demand exists here for hypocritical denials of what life has taught. In accepting evaluative characterizations of our behavior we are not being all things to all people except in the sense that we all have much in common. The point is reinforced by a distinction between the dilemma which makes Values Clarification pointless or confused and a false problem for the movement. Everything one does expresses the reasons, the ends, the values, for which one acts. Effective teaching expresses one's view of the desirability of accuracy, open-mindedness, and critical thinking. The art of teaching can thus seem inconsistent with the uncoercive formation of minds which is the obligation of educators who believe that values are outside the scope of knowledge.

As though in illustration of education's misstep into areas foreign to knowledge, Howard Kirschenbaum observes:

> [V]alues clarification ... values certain types of thinking, feeling, choosing, communicating, and acting.... Thinking critically is regarded as better than thinking non-critically. Considering consequences is regarded as better than choosing glibly or thoughtlessly. Choosing freely is considered better than simply yielding to authority or peer pressure.... If we urge critical thinking, then we value *rationality*. If we support moral reasoning, then we value *justice*. If we advocate divergent thinking, then we value autonomy or *freedom*.[27]

These "ifs" address the problem, however. If we value doing something then we must value doing it well; if we value learning then we value the virtues indispensible to it; but so long as we do not unconditionally assert that learning is desirable we avoid violating the boundary between knowledge and value.

Values Clarification is openly biased in favor of the values of liberal education – clarity, purposefulness, decisiveness, independence, honesty, and consistency, among numerous others. As long as education is an accepted social institution, stressing intellectual virtues is not a violation of neutrality as there is in supporting one side against another in a conflict. The bias of Values Clarification towards intellectual virtues, therefore, hardly warrants the complaint that it is "value obfuscating rather than value clarifying to teach such values through the back door, and at the same time to give the impression of value neutrality through the front door."[28] The boundaries of neutrality are at least as broad as the social consensus which exists on important matters. This fact draws into the legitimate ambit of Values Clarification a theme often stressed by Dewey, who insisted that students be initiated into the culture of a community – its habits, customs, values, and knowledge.[29]

The conditional justification of bias towards intellectual values is only partly successful. In order to protect the autonomy of individual choice, it includes the dubious assumption that education and other social institutions are theoretically questionable practices whose value might intelligibly be contested. However if we suppose that knowledge is a rational purpose for beings who experience curiosity and that educational practices are necessary for satisfying this need, then some form of the institution of education is inextricably tied to the imperative of learning. Commitment to the values of the institution, therefore, is not coherently provisional.

Not to recognize rational ends and the further values they explain creates impossible problems. If one goal were as good as another and knowledge were not the object of a rational desire, then the value of consistency and other educational virtues would depend solely upon the strength of an instinctoid liking. Because the instinct is weakly expressed in some persons, they would have no reason to want these virtues, and they would not regret their mental lives being fragmented by contradictions. One's sense of self would also be subject to fragmentation when the desire for consistency among one's chosen ends was only a weakly felt inclination. Under these circumstances, autonomy lacks importance, and value-clarifying discussion loses its rationale. There can be good reason to resist such forms of contradiction and dissociation only if they are thought to be contrary to a good life, but in this case discussion presupposes that there is an acceptable standard in terms of which personal inclinations can be assessed. Yet such standards are taboo for Values Clarification.

The taboo explains the undiscriminating conflation of injunctions against saying "You shouldn't like that" and "You shouldn't be interested in things like that." Likes and interests are far removed when the former constitute wants and the latter are related to needs. We often have good reasons for saying that a person ought not to be interested in something, reasons which are consistent with one's life and experiences rather than interferences in it. The criticism may be appropriate when it is an invitation to broaden one's horizons, to look more carefully at a specious puzzle, to attend to a fact that has been overlooked. In suppressing such helpful suggestions by understanding reasons solely in terms of chosen desires Values Clarification avoids preaching particular values, but it advocates a truncated and contentious theory of value. In so doing it commits the serious violation of neutrality typical of modern moral theory and subjects discussion to severe distortions.

Life-boat and bomb-shelter examples make it clear that clarifying discussion lacks the resources necessary for drawing distinctions between profoundly different kinds of reasons for choice and action. If someone must be excluded from a fall-out shelter, should it be the 31-year-old bookkeeper, his pregnant wife, the black militant medical student, the famous 42-year-old historian, or the 54-year-old rabbi? Using this kind of question as an exercise betokens inability to consider matters necessary for dealing with it meaningfully – the complex particularity of real situations, the difficulties of judgment where no general rules exist, the possibility of moral calamity, the difference between moral qualities and considerations of color, creed, age, and gender. These absent elements support a different vocation for moral education than the encouragement of autonomously fashioned schedules of choice. Practical understanding may come from consensus-generating forms of discussion which aim to fashion an acceptable interpretation of pre-existing emotional agreements. Of course, these conversations may not end in a common perception, or they may suggest that a problem cannot be solved and must simply be accepted; but they are the primary vehicle of practical reasoning. It is important that we attend to their role in shaping individual personalities and enabling agreements in a way that goes beyond choosing desires.

Much the same conclusion can be derived from another 20th-century debate. H. H. Price noted that "it came to be very widely accepted, among professional philosophers at any rate, that clarification is the fundamental aim of philosophy. Philosophy, it was often said, gives us no new knowledge, it only makes clear to us what we know already."[30] Among the objections to the clarifying trend was that "an increase in clarity will not make us more conscientious.... If we have no conscience to begin with, and no desire to do what is right, the clarifying philosopher cannot give us these things."[31] Conscience develops through the interpretation of moral emotions in cultural conversation.

II *Cognitive Development*

Kohlberg elaborates similar doubts about the clarifying trend but proposes a different solution. He raises two questions in describing the plight of a teacher who believes she should allow her pupils to formulate their own values but who is unhappy if they choose to cheat: "Do we wish students to understand that there are some universal non-relative moral values in choice situations?" and "Do we wish to influence a student's behavior or action in a definite direction as this teacher did? She wanted to get the kids to stop cheating." He answers: "The implications of the term Moral Education are that we *do*. A rather morally uncomfortable implication of Values Clarification is that we *do not*."[32]

Kohlberg's solution to this difficulty is that "in the general area of values" Values Clarification is correct. "I believe that we must adopt *a relativistic* stand about decisions, i.e., we should be engaged in developing valuing processes in some sense without worrying about what conclusions come out or what the principles used are. *But this is not the case in the area of morality*."[33] As it turns out, the area of morality does not primarily include the matters of cheating and honesty which concerned the teacher. It is defined by principles for resolving the interpersonal conflicts of interest not much considered in Values Clarification. Moral values differ from the personal preferences which are the objects of that school's clarifying techniques.

According to Kohlberg, moral judgments should be understood in terms of a hierarchy of cognitive structures expressing principles of right action. He has made his case so persuasively that leaders of the Values Clarification movement see the viewpoints as largely complementary, moral development having to do with upward movement towards new levels of reasoning, Values Clarification with improving the integration of one's life at any level. The possibility of "applying Kohlberg's ideas," is sometimes taken farther. "Values Clarification serves vertical as well as horizontal or integration purposes .... Values Clarification not only assists students in integrating their lives at current levels, but very likely introduces development-stimulating dissonance."[34]

Nothing prevents the intuitive psychology of Values Clarification from being consistent with Kohlberg's more theoretical claims. Both claim basic allegiance to Dewey, and Values Clarification would have no difficulty appropriating his references to stage development. Dewey frequently remarks that "the mind at every stage of growth has its own logic" and says that "in natural growth each successive stage of activity prepares ... the conditions for the manifestation of the next stage."[35] It is noteworthy, however, that Dewey's "stages" do not constitute a series of cognitive levels. As his description of development indicates, the process is seen as a continuous one without discrete upward steps in cognitive or moral capacity. As befits an edifying philosophy, the stages are metaphorical. We will see that this is equally true of several of Kohlberg's stages. One consequence is that many objections to Values Clarification apply equally powerfully to Kohlberg's views on morality and moral education. His complaint that Values Clarification cannot distinguish moral values from personal preferences can be duplicated in the case of his own inability to discern rational values outside of morality. His view of cognitive structures can no more accommodate the idea of emotions as rational than can a view of value as chosen desire, so that neither view can explain the desirability of knowledge, security, and recognition which is given them by justifiable curiosity, fear, and pride. As a result, if Oakeshott is right, Kohlberg's conception of moral education as "the presentation and explanation of moral principles" is "merely morality reduced to a technique."[36]

Kohlberg distinguishes six forms of practical reasoning which succeed one another in regular fashion. Few persons progress through all the stages, and the rate of progress may differ according to culture, but everyone follows the same order, and reversion to a previous stage does not occur. Those who reason at one stage may understand arguments formulated at the next higher stage and find them superior, but this preference reflects the mixed character of most persons' moral orientations – the fact that people are often in transition from one stage to the next, even though the preponderance of their judgments would lead to their still being considered to occupy the lower of the two stages. These are thus developmental stages in Rousseau's sense: claims representing a full stage or more above one's own will not be understood or will be misinterpreted as belonging to a lower stage.[37] Recent qualifications by Rest to Kohlberg's conception of stages do not alter these results in any fundamental way.[38]

Kohlberg groups moral conceptions into three levels of development – preconventional, conventional, autonomous. They might instead be taken to distinguish childhood, adolescence, and moral adulthood, except that Kohlberg wishes to avoid maturationist assumptions of a kind which he associates with the "romantic" tradition in philosophy. The successive viewpoints do not simply emerge of their own accord. Rather they define rational moral progress in that their component stages are constituted by increasingly adequate standards for resolving conflicts of interest. Higher or more developed stages are, Kohlberg believes, justifiably so evaluated because of their greater capacity for dealing with practical problems presented by one's environment and because they come increasingly close to the prevailing "progressive" philosophical understanding of the moral point of view.

While Kohlberg appeals repeatedly to the philosophical opinions of Kant, Dewey, and Rawls in defence of "the highest stage of moral judgment,"[39] he does not note how widely the idea of human development as involving a series of qualitative changes in conceptions of right action is attested to in philosophical literature. That is natural, since the immediate antecedents of his own views lie elsewhere – in the work of Baldwin and Piaget in particular – but the main ideas are pervasive. Although the classification of moral conceptions differs and the number discriminated varies among commentators, the view that there is a decided pattern of development is commonplace, and many of the three levels of two stages each which are described in Kohlberg's articles find expression by thinkers – including Plato, Hegel, and Rousseau – who might be regarded as providing the hypothesis which recent empirical investigations confirm. *Emile* provides a particularly dramatic correspondence but also a strong challenge to Kohlberg's theoretical explanation of the facts he describes.

Kohlberg's business, like Rousseau's, is to indicate the order and development of our knowledge. They share the stage-conception of development which is reflected in Rousseau's insistence that "before the age of reason it is impossible to form any idea of moral beings or social relations; so avoid, as far as may be, the use of words which express these ideas, lest the child at an early age should attach the wrong ideas to them."[40] The agreement goes well beyond a general congruence of conception to their detailed accounts of the two lower levels. It is almost as if Kohlberg had taken up the task suggested by Rousseau, who said that "Others will perhaps work out what I have here merely indicated."[41]

Kohlberg agrees entirely with Rousseau's assessment of juvenile capacities. Where Rousseau warns that "the child's sayings do not mean to him what they mean to us, the ideas he attaches to them are different,"[42] Kohlberg notes that "the child is responsive to cultural rules and labels of good and bad, right and wrong, but interprets these labels in terms of either the physical or the hedonistic consequences of action ..., or in terms of the physical power of those who enunciate the rules and labels." The initial or "stage-1" conception of right and wrong is thus a "punishment and obedience orientation" in which "the physical consequences of action determine its goodness or badness regardless of the human meaning or value of these consequences. Avoidance of punishment and unquestioning deference to power are valued in their own right."[43]

Rousseau's youth, who "values most the things which are of use to himself," has reached Kohlberg's second stage of practical reasoning, "the instrumental relativist orientation." The best action now "consists of that which instrumentally satisfies one's needs .... Human relations are viewed in terms like those of the market place." In consequence, "stage 2 has a clear sense of fairness as quantitative equality in exchange ... between individuals. Positively, it prescribes acts of reciprocity conceived as the equal exchange of favours ...; negatively, it deems right noninterference in the sphere of another, for example, 'You shouldn't hurt or interfere with me, and I shouldn't hurt or interfere with you.'"[44]

Where Rousseau speaks of Emile's new ability to "perceive himself in his fellow creatures," Kohlberg identifies the third stage of development as the "interpersonal concordance" or "good boy/nice girl" orientation. Since "maintaining the expectations of the individual's family, group, or nation is perceived as valuable in its own right, regardless of immediate and obvious consequences ... good behavior is that which pleases or helps others and is approved by them."[45] Rousseau and Kohlberg also agree that "stage 3 notions fit best the institutions of family and friendship that can be grounded on concrete, positive interpersonal relationship"[46] and that the viewpoint is inadequate for dealing with problems which arise when one's encounters with other persons increasingly involve strangers.

As Kohlberg puts it, at stage 4 morality is understood in terms of "a social *order* of roles and rules that are shared and accepted by the entire community, and that constitute the community. In terms of role taking, this means that each actor must orient to the other's orientation as part of a larger system to which they both belong, and to which all are oriented." He remarks that this "society maintaining orientation ... toward authority, fixed rules, and the maintenance of the social order" is the most common, but not the most adequate, adult morality.[47]

Rousseau stressed the importance of establishing "the rights of humanity" and "principles of political law." Kohlberg similarly maintains that if we are to deal effectively with problems regarding bad institutions and questionable authorities, we must move to a critical, autonomous, post-conventional, or principled morality. The first of the two stages on this level is a "social-contract orientation" which views right action "in terms of general individual rights and in terms of standards that have been critically examined and agreed on by the whole society."[48] Such a social-contract conception of justice overcomes the limitation of the previous stage and, by granting each individual a role in formulating, criticizing, and changing the laws, enshrines a humanistic outlook as morally one stage above the law-and-order authoritarianism of the society-maintaining orientation.

Kohlberg has sought to distinguish yet another stage, a "universal ethical principle orientation" which places abstract principles of justice, human dignity, and equality above law and contract and gives practical reasoning a universality which lower stages lack. The viewpoint focuses on the rights of humanity independent of civil society and includes a radical respect for personality and human life. However Kohlberg now reports "dropping the sixth stage as a reliably rateable stage in our longitudinal data" and suggests "it was all my imagination."[49] In almost every respect, therefore, his account of moral development and Rousseau's are descriptively equivalent. Nevertheless, there remain major differences of moral and psychological theory which are hidden behind this equivalence and which silently influence the way in which the stages are interpreted. A careful examination of these differences seriously undermines Kohlberg's account of the mechanism of development.

In postulating a developmental process marked by a sequence of distinctive conceptual reorganizations, Kohlberg rejects the behavioristic doctrines of "social learning theory," which views moral development as the internalization of other persons' norms in appreciation of the rewards of conformity. He complains that this view "assumes that the process of learning truths is the same as the process of learning lies or illusions" so that "learning" does not entail "knowing."[50] To this extent the agreement between Kohlberg and Rousseau holds, but their understanding of moral knowledge and the path to it are very different. Kohlberg views the developmental process as primarily cognitive, as consisting of a series of intellectual conflicts which lead to distinctive conceptual structures. At a given stage new conceptual differentiations lead to problems which can be resolved only by integrating these distinctions within a pattern of thought which restores cognitive equilibrium. Similar processes occur in all of the dimensions of our intellectual life, but practical reasoning is distinguished by the nature of the problems which spur development, namely perceived conflicts of interest. In Kohlberg's description of moral ascent the resolution of these conflicts displays a significant pattern of increasingly general viewpoints and disinterested modes of evaluation. The particular properties of particular individuals are increasingly subordinated to more abstract considerations and the basis of judgment moves progressively from self-interest to social approval and finally to moral principle.

The structuralist explanation of the facts of development seems at first to account for these changes very nicely. Is it desirable to steal in order to save a life if no serious harm is done to the victim of the theft? Typical stage-one answers are: "Yes, you will get in trouble if you let the person die," and "No, if you steal you will be caught and sent to jail." Either response is adequate until a person becomes able to distinguish the instrumental value of other individuals from the consequences of disobedience. Because the two criteria can have conflicting implications the problem of evaluation can be resolved only when one of them is given superior status; and since instrumental considerations provide much increased scope for practical reasoning they are inevitably ranked ahead of punishment as a standard of evaluation. There are thus two main moments to the stage transition. First a differentiation occurs which enables a stage-one thinker to appreciate and be attracted to stage-two reasoning, and then the relevant principles – punishment-avoidance and instrumental value – are ordered into the stable structure which defines the higher stage.

Similar differentiations and integrations at the second and later stages result in a sequence of "internal cognitive reorganizations" and increasingly complex moral structures. Most stage-two reasoners eventually differentiate the intrinsic value of other creatures from their instrumental value, and the new problems for choice which then arise are resolved only through a new integration in which the intrinsic importance of certain others takes precedence over their usefulness to oneself. Similarly, at stage four the value of the members of the social order is distinguished from and given priority over the claims of one's companions: it no longer seems acceptable to prefer the interests of certain people just because they are one's friends. In general, conceptual distinctions intelligible at a given stage reveal the inadequacy of that orientation and draw one to a more satisfactorily integrated set of concepts until, at the highest level, moral principles – which do not discriminate among interests according to whose interests they are – provide a structure sufficiently differentiated and integrated to resolve any problem involving a conflict of interest.

This interpretation of the facts of moral growth makes it possible to generalize upon some other observed features of the developmental sequence and to assert its irreversibility, invariability, and universality. It is in anyone's interest to devise structures with a superior capacity for resolving conflicts of interest, and since the increasing superiority of such structures is a basic feature of stage development, only serious injury or disease could cause regression to an earlier stage. The invariability of the sequence follows from the way in which moral principles derive from or are differentiated from, the lower stages of moral thought. Since "each new basic differentiation made by each stage logically depends on the differentiation before it," we may infer that "the order of differentiations could not logically be other than it is."[51] And because we are dealing here with "the logical order of moral concepts" the pattern of development cannot be subject to psychological or cultural contingencies and must be universal.

The theses of invariance, irreversibility, and universality have come under heavy criticism. Since principled thought is surprisingly rare, they seem to be unwarranted extrapolations from studies confined largely to stages two through four.[52] Invariance has been called into question by interpretations of the second-level stages as alternative rather than linear phases of development, and Kohlberg has himself wondered "whether all

Stage 6's go through Stage 5 or whether there are two alternate mature orientations"[53] as well as about the very existence of a sixth stage. It would seem that there is clear invariance only between levels – a much less exciting and controversial thesis than stage invariance. Universality has also been questioned on the grounds that many cultures display no third-level thinking, so that Kohlberg may be misrepresenting as features of moral psychology modes of thought characteristic only of constitutional democracies.[54]

These criticisms do not seem entirely warranted, for Kohlberg's generalizations are justified not only by earlier generations of philosophical observers but also by structuralist theory. If the differentiations and integrations postulated by that account explain a segment of the developmental pattern, it is reasonable to use them to predict relationships between the remaining discriminable orientations. The account is also intuitively plausible as a rational reconstruction of how we think. In either case, whether we view it as model or metaphor, the important object of examination is the structuralist picture of development.

Its advantages notwithstanding, the cognitive-structural explanation contains a conceptual lacuna which leaves it incomplete. The concept of a stage as a structured whole entails that each moral orientation is a distinct mode of thinking which organizes experience according to a characteristic problem-solving strategy. As a result, any given stage produces a consistent interpretation of all information available to it, and there is no problem which a person at that stage can understand but not solve. The cognitive conflict whose appearance means that a particular stage is no longer adequate in this sense can arise, therefore, only when conceptual differentiations occur which enable one to experience new sorts of problems. Such differentiations are thus necessary conditions of conflict and cannot themselves be explained by cognitive disequilibrium. The process of differentiation must receive an independent explanation. This is the function of Rousseau's reference to the emergence of new attitudes. The transition to stage 3, for example, begins with the emergence of fellow feeling and the identification with other persons' interests which is characteristic of pity. Such affective ties thereby incorporate a view of those interests as valid and permit a distinction between the instrumental value of other persons and their inherent value. It is the appearance of pity, in other words, which introduces conceptual differentiations and creates practical problems that are meaningless to stage-2 egoists.

For the developmental role of emotions to be clear some distinctions need to be recalled. In chapter 2 we noted a difference between empathy and pity, the first being a form of distress evoked by the perception of another's distress, the second including concern for the other and the desire to help. Empathy is interpreted egoistically – it is one's own distress which is important – and can clearly occur prior to stage 3. Only sympathy or pity introduces the ascription of value to other persons which is typical of the moral stages. There are undoubtedly important cognitive preconditions for this development, but stage-3 interpersonal concepts include more than can be identified in this way.[55] That additional factor is the assertive content of pity, the identification of unacceptable suffering in its object, without which no intellectual perspective has moral or motivational significance.[56] A similar account can be built around Rousseau's distinction between the physical and the moral elements in love.

In some respects, the explanatory role which Rousseau assigns to emotional maturation is given by Kohlberg to interaction with the environment. It is not the role of the environment which Rousseau denies, however, but its sufficiency. The conflicts between human suffering and self-interest which are presented by the environment to stage-3 reasoners are incomprehensible before the capacity for pity has aroused notions of the inherent value of other persons. A purely cognitivist and interactionist account of development is incomplete, if Rousseau is right, because only the emergence of other-regarding sentiments creates the capacity to take the role of other human beings, to accept their viewpoint as a competitor of self-interest, and to experience moral conflict between one's own desires and other persons' ends. In brief, there are affective conditions for some of the conceptual differentiations crucial for cognitive moral development.

Kohlberg does, of course, acknowledge that emotions are present in moral development. Rejecting "the assumption that cognitions and affects are different mental states," he insists that "'cognition' and 'affect' are different aspects, or perspectives, on the same mental events" and represents fear, shame, and guilt as structurally more complex versions of "the same feeling of anxiety."[57] Although this claim is metaphorically apt, it clouds matters in a way that can only make understanding relationships between cognitive and affective states more difficult. Fear, shame, and guilt are concerns distinguished by the increasingly sophisticated ideas of danger, disgrace, and wrongdoing, respectively; but while these ideas distinguish the several emotions, there is in these anxieties no affect which is recognizably "the same." Contrary to the primitive utilitarianism which would identify the "pains" of fear, shame, and guilt, it is not a matter of new conceptual differentiations and integrations building more complex cognitive structures upon a primitive feeling. Rather, the ideas in question may arise from the several different attitudes in the same way that the concept of inherent value in other persons arises from pity. Distinguishing disapproval as a motive from the practical consequences of disfavor, for example, depends upon experiencing it as shameful. Shame thus has a causal role in the development.

Kohlberg, by contrast, depicts affect as an aspect of development which "parallels" cognitive change rather than influencing it. Naturally enough, he understands Rousseau's tradition according to the same division. In his only significant discussion of that tradition, he says that the maturationist view distinguishes "cognitive and social-emotional development" as "two different things." It asserts that "since social-emotional development is an unfolding of something biologically given and is not based on knowledge of the social world, it does not depend upon cognitive growth." Rather "onset of the next stage occurs regardless of experience."[58] It is clear that this is an inaccurate depiction of Rousseau's view of development, in which affective and cognitive factors operate in intimate interdependency. His is a holistic account rather than one of independent or only contingently interacting systems. Neither the cognitive nor the affective states are primary.

The distinction between innate structures of evaluation and their social interpretation helps to explain disagreements between cognitive-developmental views and their main contemporary competitor, social-learning theory. Studies conducted from the latter standpoint appear to reveal cases of moral regression. "Children readily internalize the patterns of generosity or selfishness to which they are exposed," so that under suitable circumstances of reinforcement egoism can displace altruism. Contrary to Kohlberg, "age trends in moral judgments, therefore, are not ... the result of sequential stage development so much as they are reflections of the cognitive rules that have been abstracted as a result of modelling and reinforcement contingencies."[59] But this is a fallacious reading of the evidence, which shows not a reversion from altruism to egoism but a reinterpretation of generosity and selfishness as a result of newly altered expectations about human behavior. Rewarding altruistic behavior does not result in the internalization of a norm; rather the norm provides the interpretation of an innate standard which is not itself easily subject to the contingencies of conditioning.

Unfortunately, no such reconciliation of developmental and behavioral viewpoints is available to Kohlberg, since it depends upon a role for emotions which neither of them acknowledge. His account of the emotions is, indeed, identical to that of his social-learning opponents,[60] and it prevents him from drawing the distinction between innate emotional judgments and their social interpretation which could have enabled him to deal consistently with the facts of irrational and inhumane obedience to authority reported by Stanley Milgram and others.[61] That even individuals at the highest level of moral education will administer severe pain to other human beings is not baffling. The distinction between naturally occurring emotional judgments and the specific content imparted to these judgments by social circumstances suggests that Milgram's subjects do not set aside their basic moral convictions. Rather, under the novel circumstances of the experiment, the apparent expectations of the researcher produce an artificial distortion of the normal standards of acceptable suffering, and people temporarily acquire a deformed perception of human relationships.

The relationship between natural standards of evaluation and their social interpretation entails that the education of the emotions depends crucially on acquired knowledge and experience. Their interaction shows that it is too simple to reject the "romantic" view that "what comes from within the child is the most important aspect of development" in favor of the "progressive" view that "the organizing and developing force in the child's experience is the child's active thinking" together with "active change in patterns of thinking brought about by experiential problem-solving situations."[62] Accepting this dichotomy means that there can be no clear place for affect and attitude in Kohlberg's view of moral growth,[63] and this constraint has interesting consequences for both his moral theory and his educational views.

If the explanation of moral development requires reference to emerging sentiments of curiosity, pity, and love, then two types of moral questions arise. We may ask which of our interests are consistent with those of other persons, but we may also ask whether the interests associated with our attitudes possess the validity they purport to have. The latter inquiry is ruled out by Kohlberg, who claims that "if stages of moral judgment develop through conflict and reorganization, this is incompatible with the notion that moral judgment is a direct apprehension of natural or non-natural facts."[64] If there is no appeal to such facts, there is nothing against which the rationality of our interests might be tested. But Kohlberg's observation may be turned around into the logically equivalent statement: If moral judgment is a matter of apprehending moral facts then moral development is not simply a matter of progressive stages of structural reorganization. We seem to apprehend such facts when we experience the emotions characteristic of moral development. These experiences belong to the affective or practical perception discussed above. The course of moral development together with the deficiencies of structuralism provide additional reason for thinking these perceptions genuine.

Kohlberg has been unwise or unlucky in his choice of philosophical allies, whom he identifies in saying,

> Both psychological and philosophical analyses suggest that the more mature stage of moral thought is the more structurally adequate. This greater adequacy of morally mature moral judgments rests upon structural criteria more general than those of truth-value or efficiency. These general criteria are the *formal* criteria developmental theory holds as defining all mature structures, the criteria of increased differentiation and integration. These formal criteria (differentiation and integration) of development fit the formal criteria which philosophers of the formalist school held to characterize genuine or adequate moral judgments.[65]

Since philosophical formalists accept criteria of truth and falsity only at the level of moral principle, they subscribe to a particular and questionable interpretation of value judgments. The bias this incorporates imposes itself upon Kohlberg's views in a number of unfortunate ways. One result is an apparent misinterpretation of adolescent morality and what follows it.

In assigning sentiments no significant place in his account of development, Kohlberg not only neglects this aspect of moral growth but also makes himself liable to a mistaken characterization of stages 3 and 4. If the standards generated by sentiments are natural, then there is no level of moral reasoning which is properly called conventional. It may indeed be the case that most people follow custom and law unreflectively for part or all of their lives, but the point of *Emile* is that this limitation is avoidable. It is not an essential or defining feature of any stage of development, and respect for convention is therefore not a deep, or structural, aspect of moral development. To define stage 4 as an orientation "towards authority, fixed rules, and the maintenance of the social order," in other words, conflates the ordinary expression of a perspective with the more basic affective-cognitive capacity to respect the social order insofar as it is consistent with conscience. The descriptive agreement between Rousseau and Kohlberg remains. Both assert that there are stages in which public opinion figures importantly. They agree that public opinion commonly dominates individual conscience, so that the perspective is in this respect a conventional one. The difference is that Rousseau does not acknowledge that there is any stage in which conventional authority is an unquestioned standard.

We can, in short, be governed by nature rather than by convention, even if the one requires taking the other carefully into account and accepting law and custom when they do not violate conscience. Although conventions are inevitable aspects of our lives, we can "perceive the reasons for all the proceedings relating to age, position, and sex, on which the customs of society depend" rather than being "guided solely by habit"[66] or untutored public opinion. If this is so, then there is no developmentally necessary moral orientation which is defined by a simple strategy of following convention or in which "right" and "wrong" are understood solely in terms of maintenance of the basic rules and structures of society. The possibility of assessing the requirements of society entails that conventional standards do not constitute structural features of moral reasoning at this or any level.

The absence of conventional stages of development is consistent with Kohlberg's basic assumptions. It conflicts only with his interpretations of stages 3 and 4, and a reinterpretation might well enhance the acceptability of the theory. As Bill Puka has noted, it is necessary, in order to avoid evidence of apparent regression, to recategorize law-and-order thinking "as the ideological component of more general rationales" rather than "as criterial for stage 4."[67] For somewhat different reasons Elliot Turiel has also proposed distinguishing convention from morality.[68] Doing so has the added advantage of dispelling the problem that the course of development takes human beings through orientations which many philosophers regard as irrational.[69] The problem is not that appeal to convention is mindless – on the contrary, it involves the intelligent application of social rules to particular situations – but that it amounts to uncritical acceptance of morally questionable authority. This problem vanishes with the disappearance of conventional moral structures, that is, with suggestions that naive acceptance of rules and laws constitutes a moral stage, as opposed to often accompanying it.

If there are no conventional moral structures, it follows trivially that there is nothing properly called postconventional morality, but the loss of this distinction is not disturbing. If no stage of moral reasoning is bound by the imperatives of convention, it is not necessary to attain stage 5 before rational moral reflection can occur. A more significant implication is that the existence of a discrete stage 5 must come into question, for it now loses its main distinguishing feature – the "prior-to-society perspective" in which we assess social conventions from the external standpoint of potential participants in the social contract.[70] A prior-to-society perspective is present throughout development in the natural standards erected by basic human attitudes.

Kohlberg has in fact been considerably more ambivalent about the existence of "postconventional" stages than his original theory states. He has both suggested that "there are ... no adult stages in the structural sense" and acknowledged that only "scanty evidence" supports "the existence of adulthood cognitive and moral stages."[71] More recently, John Gibbs has argued persuasively that the final two "stages" are not structural but "existential" and that stage development in moral judgment occurs only during childhood and adolescence.[72] *Emile* provides additional reason for skepticism about "postconventional" morality. Since no new attitude distinguishes a fifth Rousseauan stage, the social-contract perspective appears to be a simple result of learning about politics.

It remains possible to distinguish what Kohlberg thinks of as the upper-level moral orientations from a morality of authority, and it is obviously important that such distinctions be drawn. Aristotle, Thomas Jefferson, and Henry Thoreau held crucially different moral positions on slavery and the legitimacy of the state, but the reality of their disagreement can be acknowledged while its proper characterization remains in question. There is little evidence to suggest that it corresponds to genuine stages of development; and it is plausible to regard the putative stages 5 and 6 as representing political ideals alternative to Kohlberg's conservative interpretation of stage 4 rather than as elements of an unvarying sequence.[73] This point is developed in the next chapter.

These facts require little change in Kohlberg's description of moral development, but they call his moral theory again into question. The formalist view suggests that moral principles characterize the logic of practical reasoning rather than the content of its conclusions. Hence, different persons may, at any given stage, resolve the same kind of conflict of interest in opposite ways, one holding, for example, that it is right to steal in order to save a life but another just as rationally denying it.[74] In the universal ethical principle orientation, the ideal of the decision-procedure sought in moral theory is more nearly realized. Kohlberg there finds refuge from idiosyncratic choices, observing that justice and respect for persons are tantamount to reverence for human life. For "stage-six" thinkers the sacredness of life is an overriding moral consideration which shows formalism to be an inadequate theory of moral value. "Stage-six" thinkers condemn capital punishment, for example, even though a contrary position does not necessarily conflict with purely formal principles.

"It is clear," says Kohlberg," that our conception of moral principle implies that one cannot ultimately separate form and content in moral analysis."[75] Formalism misinterprets moral principles and "only ends up with the old rules of conventional morality expressed in more universal and prescriptive form." Any concrete rule of action, he believes, can be universalized and thus made formally adequate, but such rules can be grotesque. Witness "refusing to tell a lie to save a human life" or "letting 10,000,000 Kulaks starve for the greater happiness of the unborn greater number." Universal rules are also inflexible. They govern types of acts in types of situations and are insensitive to the unique features of particular circumstances which may bear crucially upon questions of justice. A principle of justice must be a guide to "integrating all the morally relevant elements in concrete situations,"[76] and it is not possible to build all relevant contingencies into a moral rule.

This is an excellent statement of the need for moral judgment or perception, but it conflicts with the theory of value Kohlberg almost everywhere espouses. The problem is evident in the remarkable exception he makes to his rejection of virtues. Whereas most words for virtues are used to praise specific types of behavior, "justice" is not.

> You cannot make up behavior tests of justice as ... for honesty .... One cannot conceive of a little set of behavior tests that would indicate that Martin Luther King or Socrates were high on a trait of justice. The reason for this is that justice is not a concrete rule of action, such as lies behind virtues like honesty.
>
> To be honest means 'Don't cheat, don't steal, don't lie.' But justice is not a rule or a set of rules, it is a moral principle ..., a mode of choosing that is universal .... There are exceptions to rules, then, but no exception to principles.[77]

This appeal to principles seeks to uncover rational grounds for a substantive conception of justice. On Kohlberg's view justice requires ignoring the fact of one's particular identity and refusing to plead anyone's special case. Conflicts of interest must be resolved impartially. This becomes possible with mastering the operation of role reversal. One asks, "Can I assent to this action from everyone else's point of view?" and goes ahead only if able to do so. It is our inability ever to pursue certain courses of action consistent with this formal operation which, Kohlberg sometimes argues, leads us to identify a certain necessary content for morality, certain interests which are beyond compromise or exchange.

A man is justified in stealing a drug which will save his wife's life when a pharmacist who invented it and controls the supply asks more than he can pay, for

> the husband can take the role of the wife or of the druggist. But the druggist's claim to withhold property at the expense of a life is not reversible, he could not recognize this claim in the wife's role .... In general, then, in situations of conflicting claims, the only valid claims are those consistent with recognition of the related claims of others.[78]

However this is construed, it does not serve to span the distance between principles and virtues, even the virtue of justice. The claim of irreversibility clearly falls short if, as Kohlberg sometimes interprets it,[79] it is a description of human psychological capacities. It is only because everyone would prefer to be stolen from than to die that the option of withholding medicine does not survive the operation of reversibility. As long as interests express "instinctoid" ends, however, a hyperentrepreneurial society in which people prefer to die rather than countenance a theft is conceivable, and no fusion of form and content has been established for morality. However irreversibility might be represented as a stronger, logical constraint which does imply such a fusion and gives reasons for regarding certain social preferences as morally invalid. Such reasons can in fact be suggested. The value of life is defined by reference to emotional needs or to the meaningful ends which give life its point; but property (let us suppose) is not such an end, being only a material condition of certain needs, and it cannot, therefore, be considered more important than life. Kohlberg's philosophical assumptions, however, make such an argument unavailable to him, so that his valuation of life appears either as a mysterious intrusion into his system or as a gratuitous attempt to make good the claim that principled morality is sufficient for resolving dilemmas about right action.

Another dimension of this common dilemma for universalistic moral theory can be drawn from an interesting convergence between Rousseau's depiction of moral development in male and female and Gilligan's criticism of Kohlberg as defending a narrow and one-dimensional view of morality. Rousseau's notion that "a man has no one but himself to consider" while women are bound tightly to their social roles and relationships is related to Gilligan's observation that women construct "the moral problem as a problem of care and responsibility in relationships rather than as one of rights and rules."[80] The concern for relatedness is plausibly understood in terms of pity, love, and other relative sentiments which figure so importantly in the Rousseauan account of moral thought, together with the social circumstances which may make men less sensitive to emotional appeals. Rousseau himself was close to realizing that the characteristic differences between the moral reasoning of men and women are circumstantial in origin. Where disparate roles are not assigned to the sexes it is reasonable to suppose that neither will display one-sided forms of moral thinking. This integration requires attention to content-laden attitudes, a fact which Kohlberg struggles to discern in giving such weight to the attitude of respect for persons. The attitude and its corresponding virtue, justice, are not at all logically exceptional.

Kohlberg is rightly dissatisfied with moral conceptions defined in terms of concrete, external rules of behavior, but the theory of value he takes for granted requires him to misinterpret virtues in such terms. "Honesty" does not mean "Don't cheat, don't steal, don't lie." We do not accept as evidence of dishonesty the fact that someone steals in order to save a life. Under such circumstances it makes perfectly good sense to say that stealing is not wrong and constitutes neither grounds for guilt nor for judgments that one is untrustworthy. There are duties (e.g., paying our bills) whose rules allow little leeway and require little interpretation, but the rules pertaining to virtues are too schematic to determine when those duties are incumbent upon us. It is impossible to say in any formula-like way which acts of stealing and lying are wrong, for dishonesty is exhibited precisely by actions which violate attitudes of trust, and judgments about such violations depend upon the complex of "morally relevant features of particular situations." Questions of significance and fittingness arise here, and because such questions cannot be eliminated we must often go beyond what general rules alone can tell us about our duties.[81]

The vagueness in judgments about honesty will be missed by attending only to rules which give clear direction. Such rules closely approximate the view of honesty characteristic of "conventional morality." They can foster emotional cliches and stereotypical conceptions of virtue which do not represent appropriate objectives of moral education, so that an account of moral knowledge should recognize that mature judgments of honesty, like mature judgments of justice, require sensitivity to the system of mutual expectations which is essential for trust and respect among free agents. Given the conditions which sustain such attitudes, neither of the corresponding virtues can be identified in terms of prescribed patterns of behavior but only in terms of the perception of moral facts. Such perceptions show that Kohlberg's concern about hackneyed values is correct but that his scornful reference to the "bag of virtues" is unjustified and that his views on moral education need thorough revision.

If moral development depends in part upon processes of biological and psychological maturation, there is reason to take seriously a "fundamental principle of education" stated by Rousseau: a child "should remain in complete ignorance of those ideas which are beyond his grasp." So too for "the most useful rule of education .... Do not save time, but lose it."[82] The wise tutor delays moral lessons, lest through precocious instruction misunderstandings are planted where they can never be rooted out. In placing exclusive emphasis on cognitive aspects of development, Kohlberg, by contrast, recognizes no reason for delay. He aims to facilitate the process of development. "The goal of moral education is the stimulation of the 'natural' development of the individual child's own moral judgment and capacities, thus allowing him to use his own moral judgment to control his behavior."[83] The primary tool of such education is the moral dilemma – a problem designed to produce cognitive conflict and thereby hasten stage advance. It is not surprising that the theoretical disagreement produces a further practical one. "Do not reason coldly with youth," says Rousseau. "Let the mind speak the language of the heart, that it may be understood .... [O]ur opinions, not our actions, may be influenced by cold argument; they set us thinking, not doing; they show us what we ought to think, not what we ought to do."[84]

Kohlberg notes the same disparity between thought and action but regards it as a primary reason for seeking moral development. "Moral maturity in judgment and action are closely related .... [O]pinion or conventional belief is not virtue. An individual may believe that cheating is very bad but that does not entail that he will resist cheating in real life .... However, true knowledge of principles of justice does entail virtuous action."[85] Education for justice thus promises to bring belief and behavior into line, as well as fulfilling our moral potential and achieving the moral knowledge which is the rational objective of moral education.

It is possible to gather strong support for these propositions. Since there are internal relationships between beliefs about virtues and moral attitudes, those beliefs cannot be separated from motivation in the case of justice. Since conventional rules are external to attitudes, by contrast, they lack immediate behavioral implications. Of course, this is not Kohlberg's reasoning, and given his excessively rationalistic explanation of development it is only to be expected that the early promise of ascent has proven disappointing. He has had to drop first from the goal of attaining stage six to the goal of attaining stage five and secondly to the goal of attaining stage four. That he should do so is clearly appropriate if the fourth stage is the terminal one, but here again Kohlberg's reasoning must be different.

Kohlberg now identifies the major problem of young people as "the death called privatism," a stage-three disillusionment with legal and political authority brought about by corrupt governments and leaders. The contribution which educators can make to a solution of the problem is to provide a form of democratic schooling in which students participate actively in governing the institution. In so doing they gain a sense of public responsibility and an appreciation for political relationships not provided by other social institutions. Unfortunately, this proposition is flawed in several respects in addition to those mentioned in chapter 1.

Using Kohlberg's approach does coincide with measurable elevation of moral stage, but almost all of the discernible change has occurred between stages 2 and 3.[86] But even if most members of a class could be brought to stage 4, it is difficult to see how privatism would be overcome. From the perspective of stage 4, the typical actions of stage-5 legislators should appear to reflect stage-2 motivations. No incentive is provided, therefore, to move beyond the forums of local politics to participation in the higher levels which claim so unconvincingly to embody the principled ideal of government. Like J. S. Mill, whose view of participation Kohlberg's resembles, Kohlberg gives us little reason to be sanguine about improving political society through education.[87]

If there is any truth at all in maturationist views, this is not necessarily regrettable. Stages of development being defined by fear, curiosity, pity, and love, we need to ask what kind of capacities they represent. Since these are not political relationships, it is not clear that they will be particularly furthered by political exercises. The lessons of literature exemplified by Nussbaum's discussion of Henry James seem as well or better suited to the objectives of moral education.

The point is reinforced by a serious moral and conceptual difficulty in condemning privatism. It expresses a dubious political value, a prejudice of democratic institutions which, however defensible on other grounds, is not supported by a confirmed cognitive-developmental theory. Oakeshott clearly understands the conception of rationalist moral education which he attacks in noting that it fails in its purpose "if it has not given both ability to determine behavior by a self-conscious choice and an understanding of the ideal grounds of the choice made. Nobody can fully share this form of the moral life who is not something of a philosopher and something of a self-analyst."[88] Kohlberg put it no better in characterizing the child as a "moral philosopher" who strives to reach "principles which are articulate, comprehensive and integrated enough to be satisfying to the human intellect."[89] These agreements would be impossible if "principled morality" represented cognitive structures more complex than the stage-4 society-maintaining conception of morality defended by Oakeshott.

Oakeshott's example has two major implications for the cognitive-developmental approach to moral education. Since his understanding of moral orientations "higher" than his own shows that they are not developmental stages, it is not merely impractical but illegitimate to aim beyond stage four. It is illegitimate because to do so would be to inculcate a particular political philosophy falsely justified as expressing a more adequate cognitive structure. Because each such philosophy can be appreciated from the final stage of moral development, any preference between them must be founded upon argument and experience rather than by processes of differentiation and integration. These matters form a major part of the subject of the next chapter, as do those raised by the second implication of Oakeshott's views.

In describing the importance of learning a coherent manner of living in all its intricateness Oakeshott is suggesting the need for a wider conception of moral education than Kohlberg's. A plausible condition of being an educated person is that one display respect when respect is due, experience awe when awe is warranted, revere what is sacred, and otherwise show rational command over one's emotions. Values education then centers on developing sensitivities to the imaginative possibilities, mutual expectations, and deliberative discussions which are essential for emotional understandings. If moral understanding is instead regarded as command of principles of practical reasoning, values education shrinks to mastery of a technique for addressing conflicts of interest. This marks the failure of a theory of development: it wrongly represents political principles of right as superior to emotional judgment and as hierarchically organizable.

The extent of this failure may be estimated by once again recalling *Emile*. Rousseau was not so much interested in moral growth as in the nature of good societies. In an important sense he did not believe in moral education at all. The basic moral problem, in his view, was that our natural standards are often warped by corrupt society. This problem cannot be solved by teaching children to reason well but only by improving social environments so as to promote character. This is the ultimate practical implication of any account which views development primarily in terms of social sentiments rather than the principles of moral theory.

Chapter 5

Human Development

I   Moral Development and Political Reasoning

The pioneer of cognitive psychology, Jean Piaget, explains patterns of intellectual development in terms of a succession of mental structures arising from repeated acts of conceptual differentiation and integration.   In contrast to the conservative view that learning occurs against a background of historical prejudice, Piaget gave a central role to these formal operations in coping with novel situations and moving to more adequate ways of understanding the data of experience.   In appropriating Piaget's view and associating his formal operations with the principles of rationalistic moral philosophy, Kohlberg's theory also diverges from developmentalists like Lev Vygotsky, whose understanding of moral growth has "focussed upon the historically shaped and culturally transmitted psychology of human beings."[1]   This view identifies an interactive relationship between cognitive development and educational processes, rather than supposing that the first drives the second.

Vygotsky characterizes Piaget's "investigations of the development of thinking in school children" as assuming that "processes such as deduction and understanding, evolution of notions about the world ..., and mastery of logical forms of thought and abstract logic all occur by themselves, without any influence from school learning."[2]   Vygotsky's contrary view is that "school learning introduces something fundamentally new into the child's development," namely a "zone of proximal development." This concept distinguishes mature stages of development, identified by one's independent problem-solving capacity, from the potential stage defined by one's capacity for problem solving under the guidance of those who are more advanced. By understanding development in this way Vygotsky can conclude that "human learning presupposes a specific social nature and a process by which children grow into the intellectual life of those around them."[3] On this view schooling is not merely a stimulus to development but an integral component of intellectual growth.

The tensions between these psychological traditions easily grow into ideological warfare. On the one hand are critics of "liberal psychology" like Vygotsky. On the other are its defenders, who are sensitive to an intermediate conventional orientation between the pre-moral mode of thought and a mature outlook in which one examines social customs carefully and adopts, interprets, amends, or rejects them for reasons acceptable to oneself and others. These transitions can be variously described – in Piaget's studies of childhood moral development they are called the egocentric, heteronomous, and autonomous stages[4] – but the descriptions always tend to imply a sharp division between rationally justified morality and unquestioning obedience to social authority. They encourage a reading of anti-liberals as supporting "traditionalist and collectivist types of society," denying to young people the right, as R.S. Peters puts it, "to question the validity of their moral and political beliefs and to place any emphasis on the role of the individual in determining his own destiny." There is "plenty of scope for the attitude to rules which is characteristic of Piaget's second stage" but no encouragement for "any movement towards the autonomous stage" which is regarded as "an aberration of individualistic societies."[5] This, Israel Scheffler comments, reflects a "conception of education as an instrument of rule" rather than an activity intended "to liberate the mind."[6]

These rhetorical gambits are often accepted by Piaget's and Kohlberg's dialectical critics, who charge socio-economic bias at the foundations of cognitive-developmental schemes of explanation.[7] Since only stalemate results, our discussion of the political

146

dimension of moral reasoning will decline this style of play. It is dubious from the standpoint of a moral conservatism which discerns no dichotomy between heteronomy and autonomy, social authority and moral rationality, and even apart from this viewpoint the important distinctions between Piaget and Vygotsky are difficult to grasp. They ignore Rest's finding that people can often recognize higher Piagetan-stage claims put to them by others than they can spontaneously produce.[8] They also neglect the importance Piaget placed on peer interaction for cognitive development and interpretations of his work which suggest that "moral knowledge is constructed by the subject in collaboration with other subjects."[9] Since both sides are prepared to accept the conversational and dialogical ideal, we do better to explore that conception than to continue the war of words.

A useful starting point is the contrast between clarifying and argumentative discussion which was foreshadowed in references to Freire and Habermas and briefly drawn again in the preceding chapter. When Freire speaks of dialogical education as a synthesis of the views of teachers and students, he identifies the former with revolutionary leaders, the latter with an oppressed people; but Vygotsky's "zone of proximal development" suggests that the concepts have a more general significance. In seeking to reach a commonality of interests through communication, Freire proposes a view of discussion in contrast to which any limitation to techniques of clarification and dilemma-resolution is severely constraining.

This notion of discussion has a strong resemblance to views which refuse to tie moral education tightly to rationalistic argument. It is consistent with Diamond's characterization of *Great Expectations* as "getting the reader to attend to a child as a centre of *a* view of the world, and, more, of what is particularly and in many ways peculiarly a *child's* view of the world."[10] It is consistent also with Nussbaum's characterization of Aristotle as insisting on the importance of tragic poetry in moral education: "It can ... advance the conversation among readers ... whose aims are ultimately defined in terms of a 'we', of people who wish to live together and share a conception of value."[11] Such discussion appeals to the heart in an effort to extend the moral imagination, modifying and expanding the natural affections.

Both Diamond and Nussbaum contest the assumption of the philosophical tradition which sees an ethical text as conversing with the intellect alone. Cold argument does not work because understanding the text centrally involves emotional response. The unresolved question is how far discussion can carry us. It is often effective in resolving practical issues which arise among friends and associates, but it does not clearly address that part of modern moral philosophy which focusses on broader encounters. In particular, it may be of little use in that part of practical reasoning which resists consensus most strongly, namely in political questions. If so, then rationalistic moral philosophy retains its importance for modern societies where, Larmore argues, "system can prove more desirable than sensitivity." Modern societies have given the distinction between the public, or political, realm and the private a significance it lacked for Aristotle. In private spheres of association there is need for judgment, accurate perception, partiality, consensus; in the public realm we require impartial and predictable procedures. This explains why "the political virtue of justice should have a precision and determinacy of rules that we do not expect of other virtues."[12]

This central issue of the distinctiveness of justice is accentuated by a difference between Freire's and Habermas's conceptions of practical discussion. We earlier noted that Freire's view resembles Habermas's notion of discourse leading dialogically to the formation of "generalizable interests," but we also observed that Habermas regards this discourse as governed by logical presuppositions akin to the principles of rationalistic moral philosophy. These presuppositions appear to encourage a succession of political principles or conceptions of justice but not to reach down to the personal level of morality governed by questions of the heart. It appears that there may still be a case to be made for moral theory whose ambitions extend beyond systematizing our thinking. Such a case might also help to rescue conceptions of development like Kohlberg's from the criticism of chapter 4, for Habermas's variation on moral theory includes a reformulation of stage-development.

Kohlberg's work in moral psychology suggests a clear answer to the question why political problems resist consensus and why many political issues remain permanently unresolved. The most intractable of these questions are those whose answers express competing ideologies, and Kohlberg's studies suggest that the main political ideologies can be ranked in order of cognitive adequacy. They imply that different individuals have markedly different capacities for political reasoning and that valid positions may seem inferior or irrational to persons whose reasoning is less advanced. If we continue to assume that Kohlberg's account of moral growth is descriptively adequate in giving an accurate empirical ordering of moral orientations,[13] the basic political disagreements in democratic societies can be understood as follows: many people whose consent must be won lack the mature political understanding required for adequate discussion and debate. Arguments representing superior orientations are easily misinterpreted. A principled advocate of equality, for example, may be convincingly caricatured as simply envious to an audience unable to appreciate the reasons for egalitarian claims. Kohlberg shows, in effect, that such attacks may be honest misrepresentations rather than deliberate distortions. His preferred remedy, of course, is moral education.

This explanatory sketch is usefully contrasted and compared with a sociological perspective on the same empirical ordering. Marxists, among others, stress the effects of social structures on political argument. In traditional and hierarchical forms of social organization, the ideological perception of conventional norms as natural standards rigidly constrains practical discussion. In a system of co-operation which endorses the free competition of individual interests, the ideology of freedom makes it impossible to take egalitarian alternatives seriously and limits discussion to finding compromises rather than permitting it to generate consensus about public objectives. In both systems forms of self-deception reflect structural barriers to adequate political reasoning. On this view, as on Rousseau's, political maturity presupposes further social development.

Both of these accounts identify structural stages of development in practical reasoning. However, if psychologists are right to regard these structures as basically cognitive, then problems of political reasoning can be traced to inflexible patterns of individual development, and the obstacles to rational agreement are not simply artifacts of the system of organization. Understanding by 'cognitive' 'affective-cognitive,' Rousseau's observations confirm part of this view too well for it to be displaced by any purely sociological account, but that part concerns the moral reasoning of children rather than political thinking. It remains possible that sociological structures might shed some useful light on specifically political reasoning, and Habermas's attempts to describe interactive competencies which bring the opposing viewpoints together suggest a fruitful synthesis. The result, though, is an account which ties political reasoning to contingently changing communicative practices. It does not (as Habermas once thought) conform to a Piagetan logic of development defined by a series of irreversible stages none of which can be passed over and each of which constitutes a more successful mode of problem-solving than the one before. The following analysis attempts to show that political development, political reasoning, and political virtues are not adequately treated by normative or scientific theory. Rather, conceptions of the good and customary expectations are inescapable aspects of our understanding of political things.

Let us begin by noting that political argument is largely moral, for it aims at determining right action. Political decisions are correct only if they conform to the Aristotelian requirement of community that no member suffer unjustified domination, which is always an injustice or wrong.[14] There is *Realpolitik*, to be sure, but deliberations about the use of force without right are surrogates for political discussion, not instances of it. Like Franz de Waal's chimpanzee communities,[15] political systems can be described without employing moral concepts; but conceptions of right and justice form an inescapable part of the context of political reasoning because they are integral to the participants' standpoint and to discussions amongst political agents. It is thus Kohlberg's conception of morality as justice which makes his studies of moral development particularly important for understanding political ideologies, i.e., familiar families of political belief. (Disputes surrounding this sometimes controversial term lie outside the focus of the present discussion.)

We have had reason to question Kohlberg's grouping of his six stages of moral development into three levels – preconventional, conventional, autonomous. His original depiction of the stages makes a dual division – pre-political and political – at least as appropriate. The evaluative conceptions in the former group may be relabeled (1) physical, (2) pragmatic, (3) interpersonal. They are pre-political in lacking the systematic vision necessary for understanding the complex interdependencies of social organizations in which questions of property and justice are central. They cause practical matters to be viewed primarily in terms of what is good rather than in terms of what is right. The following representations make it clear that considerations of political justice arise significantly only with the systematic morality of stage 4.

The pre-political focus on relatively naive conceptions of the good is evident in Kohlberg's characterizations. In stage 1, we saw, "the physical consequences of action determine its goodness or badness." In the stage-2 "instrumental-relativist" orientation, the best action "consists of that which instrumentally satisfies one's own needs and occasionally the needs of others." The orientation is identical to the viewpoint expressed by Hobbes in saying that "No man giveth but with intention of Good to himselfe; ... and of all Voluntary Acts, the Object is to every man his own Good."[16] Finally, and in contrast to Hobbes's unduly restricted conception of altruistic judgment, from the stage-3 viewpoint "good behavior is that which pleases or helps others and is approved by them." One here exhibits the patterns of social relationship and motivation which involve the ascription of intrinsic value to other people and their opinions.

Although such interpersonal judgments are social, this perspective is not yet a political one. The conception of value typical of close communities is as distinct from later perspectives as from the pragmatic form of reasoning. In being based upon concrete, personal relationships, its typical issues, as we noted above, concern how to be "good girls and boys." These are not the questions of formal right and wrong which arise within a social order defined by laws. Genuine political discussion requires the comprehension of social systems, including the concepts of law and formal authority characteristic of states. While political thinking is inherently systematic, however, it differs according to one's conception of right. Kohlberg's descriptions of these conceptions make clear the appropriateness of labeling the ostensible stages of political reasoning: (4) conservative, (5) liberal, (6) egalitarian.

The impersonal law-and-order orientation "toward authority, fixed rules, and the maintenance of the social order" which characterizes stage 4 corresponds to a sense of justice as the performance of duty, respect for authority, and preservation of the basic rules and structure of society. The defining features of the stage-5 prior-to-society or social-contract orientation are "awareness of the relativism of personal values" and the recognition of individual rights. An element of "rule-utilitarianism" – the mode of assessing social norms according to their tendency to promote social welfare – also enters into this perspective. That welfarism should become a possible part of the content of liberalism in this way is not surprising, since the norms justified by utilitarian considerations have the backing of social agreement. Where agreement is lacking, however, it would seem to follow that welfare policies may lack justification. If so, stage-5 thinking can be expressed either in the ideals of fraternal liberalism or in the laissez-faire ideals of libertarianism.

This stage-5 orientation assumes a democratic social order in which people coordinate their actions to ensure that all may seek their own good in their own way. It does not, however, seem to accommodate the importance of respect for personality, at least as this is understood at the hypothetical stage 6. The liberal conception of justice stresses "equality of opportunity; that is, equality of formal liberty to attain substantive equality." Respect for personality, by contrast, embodies a sense of justice which focuses on "the rights of humanity." It implies that "equality of opportunity means a fundamental treatment of all persons as of basic human worth." Moral judgment, from this perspective, "requires substantive moral principles" which say that "all people are to be treated equally."[17]

A number of emphases mark this "universal ethical principle orientation" as an egalitarian rather than liberal outlook: the superiority of human to merely civil rights, the appeal to substantive principles of justice which limit the relativity of valid individual interests, and, of course, the strong sense of equality which characterizes it. Egalitarian conceptions of property, in particular, find support in stage-6 thinking. Whereas "private property is conceived as the core of our society" at stage 4, and as "an institutional arrangement for maximizing the welfare of the individuals who make up society" at stage 5, the "claim to life at the expense of property rights ... is a valid claim" at stage 6.[18] This highest stage expresses the "radical and substantive ... principle of justice as equity in the distribution of income and respect."[19]

Against this background of changing moral conceptions many of our impressions of political argument become more substantial. On one hand, the fact that most people are motivated by moral beliefs rather than simply by pragmatic considerations explains why politicians in constitutional regimes generally avoid intimidation and bribery. Since such appeals are usually perceived as inferior and unsatisfactory, they would tend to offend most participants in a democratic system. On the other hand, given the difficulty or impossibility of understanding claims representing developmentally later stages, the fact that stage 4 is the commonest adult morality in any modern society should seriously limit the appeal of liberal and egalitarian arguments.

According to Kohlberg, fewer than a quarter, and perhaps only a tenth, of people deliberate at stage 5 or 6. Politicians who hope to succeed must therefore make their claims largely in conservative and interpersonal terms. Egalitarians have to be continually wary of the dangers involved in suggesting disrespect for established authority and seeming to defend greed and envy. Liberals must appeal to the conventional majority without suggesting an unprincipled cynicism that could undermine their main base of active support. These problems of political communication are moderated to some extent by the evidence that people may have an intuitive preference for somewhat higher-stage claims than those they spontaneously produce. This counts against the common opinion, recently expressed by Richard Burke, that the solution to these problems includes a tendency for political rhetoric "to fall to the lowest common denominator of the community."[20] Rather, political utterances and manifestos need to include a rich concoction of claims crafted so as to appeal from both lower and higher perspectives. Kohlberg's observations thus provide interesting insights into the complexity as well as the primitiveness of much political discussion.

Nonetheless, we have already surveyed ample reasons for caution about understanding these ideological differences as reflections of cognitive capacities. The idea must be attractive to philosophical liberals and egalitarians who can claim logical superiority for their political positions, but there are explanations of these moral differences which diverge from the model of cognitive development and lack its appeal.

The argument is fairly persuasive that cognitive-moral maturation continues through stage 4: the developmental steps in that process are marked by a series of clear and sharp conceptual differentiations – instrumental value from threat of punishment, the inherent value of other persons from their instrumental value, impersonal standards of evaluation from the inherent value of associates. An inability to make any of these discriminations leaves the later ones opaque. However the much greater difficulties for distinguishing stages 4, 5 and 6 in terms of cognitive structures suggest that the several later orientations can be viewed as alternative interpretations of a single Piagetan stage. The political characterization of Kohlberg's account adds support to this thesis. No sharp differentiations mark the conservative, liberal, and egalitarian viewpoints. Any political orientation may be intelligible to those of contrary persuasion. Consider Edmund Burke's famous views on the social contract. He clearly seems to comprehend the "stage 5" orientation in saying, "Society is indeed a contract ... but the state ought not to be considered as nothing better than a partnership agreement in a trade of pepper and coffee.... Each contract of each particular state is but a clause in the great primaeval contract of eternal society.... This law is not subject to the will of those, who by an obligation above them, and infinitely superior, are bound to submit their will to that law."[21] In the absence of contrary evidence, this conservative rendering of a liberal concept should be regarded as a disagreement, not a misunderstanding. Oakeshott's and Scruton's similar treatments of the same matters further strengthen the point. Once real disputes among philosophers are taken seriously, it becomes very difficult to maintain convincingly that cognitive structures are the most significant barriers to mature political reasoning. We noted in chapter 4 that Kohlberg now regards conservative content as an ideological accompaniment rather than defining feature of stage 4, and it seems possible to say the same of other ideologies. All of them can then be regarded as expressions of the stage-4 capacity for thinking systematically.

To propose that stage 4 is consistent with several different political orientations is not to say that everyone who reaches it has political beliefs. Full-fledged political reasoning becomes possible at stage 4, but not all systematic thinkers are likely to formulate a consistent political philosophy. In this respect stage 4, like those preceding it, is non-political, and the contrary characterization only reflects Kohlberg's original descriptions. The newly-recognized independence of the cognitive structure from particular political positions is borne out by a distinction between A and B sub-stages.[22] This conception is too problematical to be discussed here, but it is worth noting that because stage 4A is authority-centered, whereas stage 4B has the liberal content of "stage 5," the current formulation of the theory cannot represent this political difference as a matter of developmental maturity.

That differences in adult moral reasoning reflect political positions rather than developmental stages is corroborated by recent empirical studies.[23] On empirical grounds Kohlberg has himself been more ambivalent about the existence of post-conventional stages than the original theory implies,[24] and even his recent realization that stage-6 reasoning cannot be adequately documented was foreshadowed by an early perception that stages 4, 5, and 6 might be viewed as "alternative types of mature response rather than as a sequence."[25] Even so, he continues in his most recent work to retain stage 5 as a "hard," or Piagetan, stage by characterizing it as a particular set of formal rationales, procedures, and operations for dealing with problems of justice. It could be said, pursuing Kohlberg's thinking about conservative content beyond his own reflections, that the alternatives between welfare liberalism and libertarianism which occur within the prior-to-society orientation constitute differences of moral and political content accompanying the principled form of thinking. Liberalism might then be regarded as a family of ideologies associated with, but distinct from, a new social-perspective level and the justice operations peculiar to it.

There are several difficulties with such an attempt to save stage 5. Firstly, it further undermines the assumption that developmental theory is relevant to political philosophy and thereby negates the primary point of trying to sustain the superiority of the prior-to-society perspective. An "association" is not a necessary connection. If there is only an association between liberal thinking and justice operations, there is no ruling out the possibility of contrary political associations. A preference for liberal society is not then justifiable on cognitive-developmental grounds.

Secondly, even if this perspective is neutral between various forms of liberalism, it is not after all neutral between generic liberal ideas and other families of political belief. In all its forms the prior-to-society perspective understands individuals as having natural rights and freedoms whose protection requires recognizing the operation of reversibility as the ultimate criterion of justice. This reestablishes the political relevance of "stage-5" thinking by contradicting the conservative idea that social norms are authoritative and that rights flow from established institutions and customary expectations. Unfortunately, this conflict of ideologies cannot by itself establish the liberal philosophy as tied to a logically discrete stage. We know only that one of the contradictory positions must be mistaken. We do not thereby know that one is cognitively superior to the other.

Thirdly, there is no other way to show the general commitments of "stage 5" to be superior to conservative views. They remain open to doubt because the political disagreement can be viewed as a contest of customs. The contractarian perspective can be seen as an expression of traditions of freedom and independence, but of traditions nonetheless and no more or less defensible than any other system of social practices or values. So seen, reasoning according to justice operations need only express expectations about acceptable argument in a liberal culture rather than the achievement of a more adequate vision. The point is strengthened in so far as the values of freedom and independence can be represented, as by MacIntyre, not as an advance but as a result of the decay of community. In sum, the status of stage 5 is debatable, and because conservatives are full partners in the debate there is no identifiable failure of understanding as there is in disagreements prompted by operating at genuinely different cognitive stages. To suggest that a social-contract perspective is superior to acceptance of a system of antecedently existing customs may only express an ethnocentric preference for one set of political values over another. Rawls's concession of the point deprives Kohlberg of his primary philosophical authority.

A significant logical consideration underlies this last problem. It is important in discussions of development to distinguish this key concept from evolution. "Development" implies progress and logical direction, whereas "evolution" (after Darwin at any rate) implies logically random adaptation to environmental contingencies. Kohlberg interprets his entire empirical ordering as requiring a developmental rather than an evolutionary explanation, but his data for the latter part of the sequence are consistent with both accounts. There is more in developmental theory than the evidence demands, which means that the changes of political philosophies expressed as stages 4 through 6 do not have a demonstrated logical order.

In order to be quite clear about this, let us look again at the view that moral philosophies and political ideologies are shaped by social rather than cognitive structures. The Marxist form of this alternative is well known and can be quickly summarized. The generation of an economic surplus and the development of states involve people in dealings with strangers and stimulate the spread of the law-and-order thinking which is needed for the settlement of disputes arising beyond the circle of kinship. Persons with whom one forms secondary relationships are then ascribed rights which identify them as fellow participants in a social system, and individuals are considered in their role of subjects whose disputes must be resolved by a higher authority. It is not consistent with political domination, however, to tolerate critical attitudes towards laws or to encourage the transfer of legislative thinking to the population at large. Myths of natural authority may serve to prevent development of standards which encourage popular government and to reinforce the need to observe the authority of existing rules.

Just as the growth of states stimulates the spread of law-and-order thinking, evolution of the market mode of organization seems largely responsible for the spread of autonomous moral thought and the social-contract orientation. The value of commodities is determined by the fact that people want them, and unless these wants can express themselves the market cannot respond. Freedom of choice as the standard of right is the appropriate ideology for such a society, and it provides the intelligible grounds for assessing and criticizing legal arrangements and for requiring the legitimacy of law to be defined by consent. At the same time, the doctrine of freedom serves to suppress the idea that there might be collective efforts made to define social purposes in the same sort of way that rational individuals define their own.

Kohlberg's finding that stage-6 reasoning cannot be documented is easily explained by such an account of social structures. In a still-capitalist society the conditions which would encourage egalitarian reasoning are not generally available. The social circumstances do not exist in which persons might be treated simply as persons, that is, as without relevant distinctions of the sorts which define familiars, subjects, and citizens. The discontents of privatism which are often observed in market society prevent seeing oneself as an effectively participating member of the human community and thus retard the growth of a standard of political justification which requires rule by consensus rather than by electoral processes and market transactions.

A small further step accounts for the paucity of stage-5 reasoning. A majority of individuals may maintain a stage-4 outlook even in a capitalistic system of organization because they have little occasion to progress beyond conservative reasoning. In spite of inhabiting a market society, most people do not act significantly in the market, engaging only in simple exchanges rather than capitalist acts. Most of us, therefore, are only shallowly imbued with the ethos of liberty, and because the rule of the market disturbs traditional ways of life we may be ready to accept authoritarian guarantees of social order. This helps to explain the finding that a society's constitutional principles can be morally in advance of a majority of its citizens. "A sociopolitical system based on Stage 5 premises can move in a direction of moral progress even though the bulk of the members of the system and even sometimes its leaders may be Stage 4, or conventional."[26] At each point in this pattern of explanation social structures serve as well as novel cognitive capacities.

While the available data seem as consistent with this sociological account of political philosophies as with the psychological one, they again fall short of sustaining a form of developmental theory. Orthodox historical materialism represents social stages as "hard." Each social stage has its distinctive ideology, its characteristic criterion of acceptable argument which presupposes the previous viewpoint and prevents appreciation of those still to come. It is difficult to reconcile this claim with the fact that in all civilizations there have been partisans of every political philosophy. Individual capacities for such thinking are not strongly determined by forms of social organization. A social "stage" may define a predominant public philosophy, but the appeal of certain standards only shows that they have a functional role in a society's survival, not that they reflect Piaget's criteria for stage-development. The pattern of succession is logically loose and suggests evolutionary adaptation rather than structural change.

To sum up, there are reasonable psychological grounds for maintaining the existence of pre-political stages of moral development, while features of socio-economic evolution are largely adequate to explain the dominance of particular political convictions during particular historical periods. Seen in this way, the accounts provide complementary and consistent explanations of changing patterns of moral thinking. Moreover, although neither shows that the changing political viewpoints of individuals and cultures follow the Piagetan logic of development, they agree in holding that each type of moral reasoning has its own standards of rational argument. This leaves open the possibility of connecting pre-political and political reasoning in an account of the acceptability of standards which is more potent than either explanation by itself – not quite developmental, but not merely evolutionary. Habermas's attempt to unite processes of cognitive and social change within the single framework of communicative competencies is a promising beginning. Its incomplete success provides enhanced understanding of outstanding issues between rationalistic moral theory and conservative moral philosophy.

II *Between Development and Evolution*

Communicative competence may be defined as the ability to reach agreements according to justifiable standards of rationality. Since such standards define particular political philosophies, it should be possible to derive an ordered series of philosophical positions from an ordered series of such competencies. It should also be possible to envisage an advanced form of communication in which open discussion leads to social consensus in the manner of debate in small associations. This possibility lies outside those perceived by Kohlberg in limiting the use of "moral" to "judgments involving deontological concepts such as right and wrong" as opposed to "conceptions of the good, the good life, intrinsic value or purpose." Habermas seeks to go beyond this stage-6 position and its "monologically applicable principle of generalizability" to a "communally followed procedure of redeeming normative validity claims discursively."[27] This represents the derivation of a seventh stage – the universal ethic of speech – from mature communicative competence. If this were to succeed, we would have overcome the restricted view of morality which limits moral and political reasoning to resolving conflicting claims. Agreement on common purposes need no longer be only a fortunate accident, since a credible conception of the good would once again be available.

Reflected in social practice, such a derivation would move humanity beyond politics in Kohlberg's sense. Politics and criteria of right and justice are necessary as long as unresolvable conflicts of interest are normal, but when such conflicts can be settled through agreements on objectives a post-political form of human organization is in view. Habermas's distinction between stage 6 and 7 could be designed to reflect this movement beyond politics, since it describes two stages of egalitarianism distinguished by Marx in his *Critique of the Gotha Program*: the first is marked by an equality enforced through political authority, the second by equality preserved through the will of persons collectively deliberating without the intervention of the state.

Unfortunately, these possibilities and designs are weakened by the difficulty which afflicts all structuralist accounts of changing political viewpoints. In attempting to demonstrate that Kohlberg's sequence of moral stages can be derived from stages of "interactive competence," Habermas becomes vulnerable to the problem that the developmental sequence may actually terminate at stage 4. If what appear to be genuine stages can be viewed as merely an empirical ordering of political philosophies, then the kinds of interactive competence from which they are derived also lack a demonstrated logical order. Liberal and egalitarian ethics cannot be said to be inherently superior to the concrete morality of social groups without further reasons, and lacking these reasons we cannot identify the directional changes which distinguish genuine development from evolution in society or personality.

The problem persists only as long as the sequence of interactive competencies is required to conform to the model of "hard" stages. As Piaget always recognized, and as Habermas now realizes, this is an unwarranted condition.[28] It is also unnecessary. By understanding interactive competencies in terms of social practices rather than hierarchical structures we can define a pattern of change in political discourse which reflects the changing needs of intricate human organizations rather than imposing a logic upon a succession of dominant philosophies. Even if stage 4 is the most comprehensive cognitive structure, we can then identify the series of political interpretations of this structure in a way which permits saying that it constitutes development, albeit in an extended sense.

Habermas once pointed out that the practice of rational argument is commonly thought to have begun with the separation of philosophy from myth and the emergence of the polis from associations based on kinship.[29] New rules of discourse developed and created the expectation that the conclusions of discussion should conform to criteria of open dialogue and deductive validity. The differentiation of experimental science from philosophical cosmologies marked another important transition, and expectations about empirical evidence became central to the appraisal of many arguments. Practices of empirical inquiry were supplemented in turn by the institutionalization of discourse in which practical questions and political decisions were supposed to be democratically questioned and tested.

Each of these communicative practices constitutes the growth of an ability which is important to a certain level of social complexity. The appearance of philosophy marks a new social capacity for arriving at acceptable conclusions by using logical rules, a prerequisite for any constitutional form of government. The scientific revolution reflects the appearance of a further capacity to reach agreements by using the rules of empirical inquiry. Its occurrence can hardly be separated from the freedom of action and investigation essential for the rule of the market. Principled political discussion coincides with a capacity for mass democracy, and the rules of the universal ethic of speech represent a further capacity for reaching practical agreement beyond the reach of now-established practices of communication. This last capacity may not become institutionalized unless new social circumstances demand it, but it clearly illustrates the connection between a mode of social organization and accepted standards for the validity of arguments and decisions.

This series of practices indicates how a theory of communicative competence can be described independently of structuralist suppositions. For a communicative practice to become established, the cognitive capacity for it must already exist. The problem facing any such practice is not that of gaining intelligibility but that of gaining and maintaining currency. This is a matter of entrenching rules of argument and the expectations they generate, of institutionalization rather than structural development. Hence, to represent extensions of practical reasoning as tied to social practices in this way is to detach them from stages in the standard sense. We are dealing rather with a variety of ways of employing the cognitive capacity for systematic thinking.

The process of interpreting cognitive capacities does not logically justify preference for any particular political orientation but only reflects the fact that one set of argumentative practices has prevailed over others. However the way in which this happens is important and may justify a preference in a weaker sense. If Habermas is right, the historically changing capacity for communicative practices is explained by the functional needs of social organizations, and the forms of communicative competence required by more complex types of organization are desirable in reflecting and protecting existing ways of life. This is not to show that liberal and egalitarian institutions are inherently superior to other communicative possibilities, since, as far as is known today, all post-mythopoeic practices operate on the same cognitive level. It does, however, place them within a framework of change which is not merely evolutionary, assuming that they do have the direction suggested by increasing social complexity.

This direction is not guided by a compelling logic of development. Where a new communicative practice arises no unimpeachable criteria of success require a preference for it. The gain is always achieved at an expense, which may persuade some to challenge the way of life it makes possible. The differentiation of philosophical from mythopoeic thinking created enhanced capacities for logical argument, but it also meant a loss of unity and intimacy with gods and nature. The differentiation of empirical inquiry from philosophy meant a tremendous gain in capacity for experimental reasoning, but at the expense of revealed religion and the "natural ties" which bound inferiors to their superiors. Democratic political thinking creates the possibility of a self-determining society, but it requires forms of public participation which threaten some powerful interests and impinge upon the pleasures of privatism. It is because this loss may seem to outweigh any gain that conservative political thinkers do not believe that making decisions through critical and open public discussion is a desirable or even possible mode of problem solving. Too many people will take part in practices of discourse which are governed by other standards. This voluntaristic aspect of social practices entails that patterns of communicative competence are not irreversible, being subject to opposition by various general conceptions of the good and thus subject to decay from non-conformity.

Structural and institutional matters are not sufficiently distinguished in Kohlberg's latest writings, where he returns Habermas's earlier compliment of appropriating the other's work. When Habermas suggested that Kohlberg's six-stage scheme could be supplemented by distinguishing between "monological generalization" and public standards of discourse, Kohlberg replied by insisting that the use of justice operations like ideal reversible role-taking is perfectly consistent with the notion of actually engaging in dialogue. It obviously is, but the process of imaginatively putting oneself in another's position and the process of having a discussion governed by social expectations are strikingly different – so much so that it is a puzzling further claim that the "Stage 6 reasoning procedure logically requires dialogue in actual, real-life moral conflicts."[30] To say that dialogue is logically compatible with a mode of thinking is one thing; to say that it is logically required is quite another. The one is subject to empirical confirmation, the other is *a priori* speculation which runs up against contrary speculations.[31]

Kohlberg's assimilation of Habermas's seventh stage of communicative competence resembles interpretations of Piaget which emphasize the importance Piaget placed on peer interaction for cognitive development. The point to stress about such interpretations is the respective roles of cognitive and social factors in the process of construction. This relationship seems best understood in terms of the difference between the abstract conceptual capacities which define each true developmental stage and the concrete interpretations placed upon them amidst changing social practices and the expectations they generate. Such developments are "soft."

As a form of interaction, discussion plays a most important role in interpreting the cognitive structures which arise, at least in part, from other causes. Discussion influences what a stage-3 reasoner considers to be worthwhile, but it does so by shaping one's standards of behavior towards persons whose interests are seen as valuable in themselves. Such interpretations can differ widely, since discussions arising under different circumstances will lead to different conceptions of what should be tolerated; but this point can be articulated only when cognitive capacities are distinguished from the effects of social contingencies upon them. Discussion affects our understanding of the conceptual content of stage-3 judgments; it does not appear to be logically necessary for the existence of the capacity. So, too, for the role of discussion in shaping the political content of systematic reasoning. Political discussion presupposes the existence of this cognitive structure but is compatible with its conservative, liberal, or egalitarian interpretation.

As represented here, Habermas's conjoining of the Piagetan and Marxian understandings of human development demonstrates that political reasoning, and Kohlberg's ordering of stages 4 through 6, should not be understood in terms of cognitive or social structures alone but also in terms of communicative practices which embody public standards of judgment. Since the possibility of new practices of political reasoning clearly exists, it makes sense to seek "to loosen up the existing form of social integration by embodying in new institutions the rationality structures already developed in world views."[32] This is a prescription, however, not a requirement upon those who find the existing form of social organization agreeable. Within any set of institutions, including those of political discourse, there are competing interpretations. In the absence of structural foundations for these interpretations, they represent equally intelligible political preferences. What governs these preferences is a central question in the study of human development, but the answer will show that there is no panacea in either moral education as Kohlberg conceives it or in social change as Marxists conceive it.

Conceived differently, moral education and social change remain focal points of an account of development. This account will take seriously the origin of moral ideas in emotions, the imaginative extension of these ideas through social interaction and philosophical reflection, and the intimate relationship between emotional objectives and central social institutions. It will necessarily refer to the important but imperfect ability of writers and speakers to articulate and sustain a compelling picture of human relationships and varieties of the good life. In so doing it will encourage sensitivity to the common features of all human relationships and the uniqueness of every relationship resulting from each person's particular place in the vast network of lives. It will also display the ways in which this network itself can be changed through the exercise of moral imagination. One result will be to reinforce the superiority of moral conservatism over moral theory, for the account subsumes rationalist moral philosophy under a description of traditions of rational reflection, including those corresponding to the commonest political ideologies.

III Imagination in ethics and politics

From the perspective of moral conservatism, there are traditions of rational acceptability rather than a sharp contrast between reason and tradition. Reflection and argument are not exercises of pure reason but practices, or sets of practices, which can be described by their evolving rules. These traditions are not bound by iron rules of custom, as is shown by the changing requirements of rational consensus through the historical emergence of new modes of inquiry and political ideologies. Amidst such processes we apply reflection and argument both to our individual lives and to the social circumstances which exist independently of any individual. Baier and Nussbaum give many examples of this role of reflection in one's personal existence. Walzer and MacIntyre examine its place in the public sphere of life. It is an appropriate task of moral philosophy to assess attempts to recognize and interpret connections among this variety of facts.

Oakeshott honors eccentricity as an exercise of freedom and inventiveness which is sensitive to a tradition and remains faithful to it. This kind of imagination gives expression to the possibilities of behavior consistent with prevailing institutional forms, thus approving habits of criticism which seek to sustain a reflective but dynamic equilibrium. It suggests that an appropriately mixed form of the moral life would not only exhibit "the confidence in action which belongs to the well-nurtured customary moral life" but also "enjoy the advantages that spring from a reflective morality," including "the power to propagate itself beyond the range of the custom of a society."[33]

This is a very different thing from the activity described by Hampshire in asking whether we should "subject every institution around us, and every loyalty thereby engendered, to constant rational scrutiny and criticism."[34] The moral conservative must clearly reject this form of critical reflection: it interferes with the customary understanding and application of ethical terms, corresponding to the line of thought leading from the uncodifiability of moral concepts to the extreme conclusion that there is no knowledge of the good. It is less clear whether moral conservatives need reject what Lovibond calls "the (reasoned) pursuit of change [which] demands that we intervene, from time to time, in the practice which constitutes the approved use of certain sensitive terms."[35] This injunction recognizes the dynamics of living institutions. It suggests progressive possibilities for moral conservatism lying between incessant skepticism of everything artificial and the unselfconscious modifications to behavior endorsed by traditionalists.

So described, these progressive possibilities are faithful to the holistic alternative to rationalistic moral philosophy and to an unbroken tradition of philosophical thought. Even innocent Socratic questioning is intervention in a practice of approved uses. It can upset comfortable parochialism and lead to literal disillusionment with existing institutions. But it will fail to achieve a prior-to-society perspective on human reality. It is possible to question any existing practice or institution; it is not possible to repudiate the place of these customary authorities en bloc or to offer internally compelling reasons to reject an existing way of life in its entirety. Nonetheless, questioning and approval are opposing tendencies, so that it is not instantly clear what equilibrium points exist between them to define a possible form of reflection.

The opposition occurs between intellectual freedom from parochial conceptions and the kind of local knowledge which distinguishes particular communities. Its ideal resolution would permit all bodies of local knowledge to find harmonious expression within an illusionless worldview. This is certainly possible if conceptions of virtues, purposes, and obligations constitute practical knowledge which is not subject to refutation. Expressing the substance of human relationships, they are subject to reinterpretation, but they can survive inquiry because they entail no propositions which could be successfully controverted. By contrast, philosophical reflection can effectively question prevailing ideologies – the myths of superiority and necessity which legitimate the dominance of certain classes or interests. While they include criteria of agreement, a view of rational consensus, they are vulnerable to contradiction, for they questionably suppose certain patterns of relationship to be necessary when they do not have to be so regarded. Hume and Wittgenstein showed that many supposedly necessary connections – as between events and causes, rules and actions – were undemonstrated.

This pattern of philosophical reflection works on criteria of agreement as well, potentially weakening them.

Practical knowledge which includes no claims about how things must be is not threatened by this kind of philosophical examination. It is more seriously challenged by encounters with alien practices which upset previously reasonable expectations, weaken former habits of behavior, confound old customs, and encourage reinterpretation of emotional judgments. These effects are well expressed by philosophical theories. In viewing people impartially, modern moral theory raises the skeptical question why we should feel the obligations of children, husbands, employers, and other special social relationships. These moral practices are permitted from the detached point of view, but they are not required; and by regarding personal attachments as objects of moral preference the rationalistic perspective mirrors the disruptability of filial, sexual, and analogous moralities. Conservative theories, by contrast, mirror the inertia of customary moralities. They make no sharp distinction between ideology and moral knowledge, regarding myths of domination and the inventions of moral interpretation as alike necessary to the integrity of communities. Since this anti-rationalism is vulnerable to reflection, the liabilities of ideology infect moral knowledge, leading easily to the view that no coherent moral practices remain. In its own way, conservative theory also expresses a diminished sense of moral belief.

When philosophical theory is put aside, philosophical reflection becomes a more potent critical instrument. Recognizing that moral concepts are subject to a variety of practical interpretations and cannot properly claim indubitability, its incompatibility with moral absolutism enhances the chances for free discussion. Recognizing that morality is not a seamless web in which the failure of any part would mean the failure of the whole, it can appreciate that the conflicting and overlapping dispositions, practices, and principles which make up a culture's moral outlook can each provide a partial and tentative perspective for the criticism of the others. One result can be an interest in developing new institutions, like Habermas's in a society whose course of development is determined democratically rather than resulting from countless private interactions and executive decisions. Canvassing this issue can give greater definition to the reflective dimension of moral conservatism.

We immediately encounter an opposition between the totalistic vision of a society governed by consensus and the pluralism of the conservative argument. It does not seem inherently mysterious, however, to contemplate democratic forms of moral reflection. There is a first-person plural view as well as a first-person singular one, and it makes sense to speak not only of reflective persons but of reflective societies in which fundamental alternatives are actively explored, debated and decided upon. The result would be collectively generated expectations about the future, a sense of the social good. This is the outline of a communitarian sense of politics in which the essential place of traditional norms would be filled, in part, by a tradition of open decision free of overt emotional appeals. Certain kinds of agreement would be considered valid only if reached in this way. An institutionalized practice of consensual decision-making would entrench understandings and norms of argument which fulfil a conservative function.

In any conservative form, an account of communicative practices will be anti-rationalistic, embracing fictive realities rather than seeking secure foundations. People bring to a common exploration of social possibilities only the abstract purposes typical of the emotions which create a shared form of moral life. This primary agreement is complicated by the diverse conceptions of goods which result from differences of individual circumstance, training, temperament, and disposition. These particular interests may lack demonstrable validity when contests between them occur: argument alone cannot resolve differences among such conflicting notions. Nothing will do but a decision of the kind which regularly faces any corporate body in which a variety of alternative possibilities vie for acceptance. Where such bodies function well there are recognized practices for choosing among competing views, and when the practices are followed the outcome becomes the will of the whole. Some preferences are disappointed but the use of deliberative processes accepted as valid leads to the creation of common purposes.

Much of this interplay between reflection and decision is evident in legal reasoning as portrayed by Ronald Dworkin's alternative to legal positivism. On the positivists' model, valid judgments follow logically from basic legal norms and the facts of a case. When these facts do not fall under a single, clear legal rule, and where no clear procedural canon is available to deal with this indeterminacy, judges must simply exercise their discretion. Dworkin objects that this account is unfaithful to the actual practice of legal adjudication, which does not reflect the stark alternative between the application of valid laws to particular cases or the use of discretion. Judges never step beyond the law and adopt the role of legislator. They are constrained by the complex tradition in which they are hermeneutically situated. Judges' decisions are interpretations of existing law, and their correctness is determined by the extent to which their judgments are seen as meaningful in the light of legal history and tradition. Seen in this way, legal reasoning shares many features of reading and criticizing novels and other literary texts.[36]

Political practices in a modern democracy resemble one extreme of the positivist's account of legal reasoning. Arguments are made and votes are taken, but since the arguments do not dictate the outcome the discretion of the majority determines the decision. A possibility more akin to the hermeneutical model was suggested just above. Important abstract goods – security, provision for the needy, knowledge, and the like – motivate social debate about shelter, welfare, education, etc. To decide public policy in such matters is to fix interpretations of abstract goods for a time: minimum standards of housing will determine expectations in terms of which security is understood, welfare policies define notions of when suffering is not to be tolerated. In arriving at a policy, a contestable abstract good is thus given a particular interpretation which settles its public meaning in the same way that traditional patterns of housing and provision settle such meanings in unreflective societies.

We have many examples of these processes. When freely contending parties offer their proposals in the setting of electoral confrontation, no side will gain unanimous support. The outcome can nevertheless be decisive as long as the debate concerns competing visions of the social good. Because they are open to interpretation, politically salient concepts like security, relief, liberty, and equality are natural loci of competing viewpoints; but when a decision is made an interpretation is, in principle, fixed. It is not simply that a policy is chosen; an abstract good is given a particular social meaning which even those on the losing side can accept. They do not get what they would have preferred; but no one's rational purposes are denied, there being no such purposes prior to the contestable abstract good's being given a particular interpretation. Thereafter, the social facts sustain certain rightful expectations although other viewpoints doubtless continue to exist.

In order to illustrate this process, suppose that public argument leads a government to remove the personal cost attached to medical attention. Individuals then have reason to expect protections they did not previously enjoy. This gives new meaning to the concept of security, and because security is undeniably a good, the validity of expectations of medical service becomes generally acknowledged – even by most of those who argued against public health measures on the grounds that they undermine other values or that social resources could be better expended. Opposition is entirely reasonable as long as the interpretation of security remains unsettled. It is possible but less reasonable once the matter is decided by a valid political decision. A rational purpose is then created and makes a claim superior to any desires which lack the support of good reasons.

Because nascent forms of these processes are familiar enough, the prospect of a reflective and self-determining society does not seem absurdly remote. Communicative practices as described here are not too abstract to function in a manner analogous to established customs. The possible objects of human desire are not so various that moral ways of life incessantly conflict. Moral languages do not prove incommensurable, precluding significant discussion. The inherent contestability of crucial concepts does not always frustrate agreement. The constraints established by natural agreements obviate the corresponding doubts. Given the common conceptual framework established by human psychology, it is possible to envisage the creation of common conceptions of the good even within pluralistic civilizations.

This account of publicly determinable rational purposes is both pluralistic and holistic. It recognizes the permanence of contention, choice, and a diversity of goods while at the same time describing the possibility of a normative totality of generalizable interests or communicatively-shared needs. It also suggests a sense of politics consistent with modes of social decision acceptable to Marxists. Social measures enacted after long public debate are implementations of the social will rather than impositions of political leaders. They exemplify a mode of social development which could be strengthened by encouraging institutions of public debate and decision. By providing access for ordinary people to influence legislative discussion, by opening up the ownership of mass media, by extending the issues subject to collective bargaining, and in many other ways, new and deeper expectations about popular sovereignty would develop. Since there is no predicting the outcome of unconstrained public discussion, this is a picture of politics as a means rather than as a program to be introduced.[37] In this respect it remains politically neutral.

The suggestion that there might be reflective societies as well as reflective individuals is thus consistent with the anti-utopianism of moral conservatism. It simply depicts a possible state of affairs. It does not describe how such a democratic community might be brought about or establish any likelihood that one might arise. Philosophical speculation does not have the capacity to change society, but philosophers can be interested in defining new avenues of interpretation which partisans of a point of view can use in trying to persuade others to perceive things in their way. In such intellectual contests there is no preordained victor. The form of deliberation imagined here expresses one interpretation of a free society. It has no preferred place over alternative interpretations but defines a sense of freedom which, by the above argument, can become rational only if consensual modes of decision become normal.

The passions and social institutions form the center of the conservative intellectual tradition. By interpreting them in terms of moral beliefs and progressive institutions, the resources of this view of the moral life can be seen to include unexpected possibilities. The existence of these possibilities undermines the strongest objections to conservative conceptions of practical reasoning. The conditions of interpretation are consistent with internal criticism and change. They are not consistent with a culturally presuppositionless critique of our society or the prospect of a break between interpretation and practice. Thus, although Richard Bernstein plausibly speaks of a principle of dialogue or conversation as "a powerful regulative ideal that can orient our practical and political lives," he calls less convincingly for "a form of argumentation that seeks to warrant what is valid" in a tradition.[38] Rather we need to understand that patterns of emotional response modulated in personal monologues and in conversations with others provide us the only grounds of evaluation available.

Conclusion

The limitations of rationalistic conceptions of human moral development suggest that moral philosophy is better able to improve our understanding when it examines moral practices than when it pursues moral theory. Practices of moral reflection and argument – ranging from literary invention to political persuasion – include everything we can reasonably hope for in seeking to fashion a sense of our personal good and responsibilities and to resolve disagreements about desirable public arrangements. The rational acceptability of assertions and demands is not determined by permanent principles but by evolving patterns of expectation. Reasons and customs reflect one another.

The inadequacies of rationalist moral theory are evident in many places, including the problems and confusions of contemporary views of moral education. We have seen that the doubts about goods and virtues typical of these views do not preserve a place for rational choice but call it too into question. This quandary is best addressed by acknowledging the central role of emotional rationality. The emotions do most of the work expected of rational principles without imposing an impossible burden on "reason alone." The education of the emotions can have all of the integrative effects valued in our culture, promoting whole, aware, and responsible persons.

Our emotions locate us in time. We regret certain things about the past and have hopes for the future. In so doing we make evaluations which give definition to a self. The tendency, much examined by philosophers, to prefer immediate benefit to deferred gratification reflects a foreshortened notion of self, inhibiting the formation of a sense of one's whole life. It is a conspicuous feature of the education of emotions that it tends to result in more ample self-conceptions. Reflection does not identify better reasons for preferring the present or almost-present to one's future good, and when this abstract recognition is coupled with literary and historical examples of interesting lives, one may be motivated to explore and to push back the boundaries of one's concerns, thus becoming interested in the whole course of one's life.

It is notable that this appreciation of self does not rest on logical demonstration but on the growth of powers of hope, prudence, and regret. Hope gives future states of affairs a claim upon one's attention and extends the field of practical deliberation. In involving a conception of the person not driven simply by blind impulses and the preferences they motivate, it belongs to a structure of aspiration characteristic of self-directing agents. Since this structure is also a fact of psychology rather than rational will, many contingencies can impede its expression. Natural and social circumstances affect one's knowledge and control of future events, thus shaping one's expectations. Where these circumstances do not support long-term expectations the conception of self may be narrow, but where we are in greater command of our environment it can be expansive.

Emotions also locate us directly among other persons. Pity makes claims which raise questions that cannot otherwise be asked. In contrast to empathic responses, it asserts the importance of other people or animals and raises the question whether other creatures warrant our attention when they suffer. This is not a question which can be answered by careful observation or by a personal decision to regard suffering as a bad thing but only by rationalizing the relationship established by pity in much the way that we construct a conception of a life, the self through time. We are concerned for our own suffering, but no convincing argument favors concern for it over that of others. Inclinations to prefer one's own case are thus called into question by the natural voice of compassion. Competing voices may still be louder, but where clear norms distinguish selfishness from self-interest, excessive from acceptable suffering, and the like, we can discriminate occasions calling for altruism from those which do not. This extension of our capacities is furthered by models from history, literature, and present example. Without these models one is likely to be confused or cold, so that here too the success of education depends on one's surroundings as well as on imagination.

Love – the exogamous emotion – connects us with other communities. Rationalizing this relationship and adding a political identity to prudence and altruism, we have seen, can find expression in any of several ideologies. Realizing that none of them is uniquely sanctioned by rational moral principles may dampen utopian zeal and encourage philosophical detachment from the struggles of one's society; but it may also expand our sense of moral and political possibility. There is a clear role for moral education which gives central place to patterns of communicative and interpretative action and leads beyond the morality of close associations. Such education promotes the capacities to talk and listen which enable us to entertain and to offer imaginative creations in such a way that they have the chance of becoming institutional realities. It encourages serious and enthusiastic pursuit of political goods and the rights they require while recognizing that they are always tentative and ultimately groundless.

Whole territories on the border of moral education remain to be surveyed. Aesthetic emotions open education to possibilities for perception permitted by replacing vague or crude sentiments with more specific and discriminating ones. Aesthetic education can assist in shaking us from emotional prejudice and sentimentality, providing an understanding of things which the accumulation of information cannot do. Of course, if art can be educative it can also be subversive or indoctrinative, and understandings can also succumb to excesses of subjectivism when social capacities for reaching agreements are weak. These familiar difficulties are identical in form to those encountered in moral perception. If, at least, the framework for thinking about moral questions which occupies the greater part of this essay proves useful, it will apply as well to aesthetic as to moral judgments, some reflecting purely personal responses, others being expressions of more developed attitudes subject to norms of validation.[1] We can say too that knowledge of systems of musical, painterly, and literary composition – and of the plurality of these systems – provide the ingredients of the higher education of aesthetic emotions. This can lead to speculation about competing theories of art, but questions about the role of theory in aesthetics have been as effective as the assault on moral theory.[2]

Human beings also experience religious emotions, and it is difficult to avoid the conclusion that religious beliefs display the same patterns of development and educability as moral and aesthetic beliefs. In this case, it would seem, a community can have a legitimate educational interest in promoting such beliefs, especially when they include none of the ontological or ideological commitments which are subject to philosophical criticism. A reverential attitude towards nature, for example, might justifiably distinguish ways in which the natural environment can be put to human use and ways in which it cannot. To misuse nature would then be a clear mistake, but not a prudential, moral, or aesthetic one – not prudential because making no reference to self-interest, not moral because nature is not subject to animal suffering, not aesthetic because the mistake is not limited to appearances. While it is important to note the similar features of such various judgments and attitudes, nothing is gained by trying to assimilate them to a single family, as Kohlberg does in understanding aesthetic and religious themes in moral terms.[3] A virtue of Kohlberg's comparison, however, is that it allows us to see the systematic questions about our place in the universe as having competing theological theories as answers. There is a "stage-4" view of the universe as a product of design, a "stage-5" view of God in terms of "the self as always directed towards the infinite," and a "stage-6" "cosmic" standpoint which recognizes no duality.[4] Since the competition among these theories is not finally resolvable, no side can claim the knowledge which is the aim of education.

Conclusion

This picture of good lives and moral education is one in which the possibility of moral certainty disappears but the possibility of moral confidence and tolerance remains. Moral beliefs, together with other expressions of emotional perception, are subject to question because of the scope for interpretation allowed by emotional concepts, but the view of moral philosophy expressed here implies that agreement is also possible. At the same time, because nothing requires agreement, confidence in our own convictions and traditions does not depend upon refuting contrary views. Having good reason to think that the permanent features of emotion will make the future of moral discourse much like the past, we can welcome our differences as long as we remain able to talk with one another and with ourselves.

NOTES

Introduction

1. This argument is pursued in Stanley G. Clarke and Evan Simpson, eds., *Anti-Theory in Ethics and Moral Conservatism*.

2. Aristotle, *Metaphysica*, 980^{a}21, 982^{b}12-14

3. David Hume, *Enquiry Concerning Human Understanding*, p. 83

4. R.S. Peters, *Psychology and Ethical Development*, p. 286, and Stephen Toulmin, "The Tyranny of Principles," p. 31

5. Alasdair MacIntyre, "Moral Philosophy: What Next?," in S. Hauerwas and A. MacIntyre, eds., *Revisions*, p. 9

6. William Empson, *Collected Poems*, pp. 32-33

7. W.B. Yeats, "The Second Coming," in his *Collected Poems*, pp. 184-185; Alasdair MacIntyre, *After Virtue*, p. 245

Chapter 1

1. Dwight Boyd and Lawrence Kohlberg, "The Is-Ought Problem: A Developmental Perspective," p. 360

2. L. Kohlberg, "Why a Higher Stage is a Better Stage," quoted by Dwight Boyd, "The Moralberry Pie," p. 71

3. Carol Gilligan, *In a Different Voice*, p. 73

4. Ibid., pp. 7-8. Also see Virginia Held, "Feminism and Epistemology: Recent Work on the Connection Between Gender and Knowledge."

5. Christina Hoff Sommers, "Filial Morality" and Stuart Hampshire, *Morality and Conflict*, p. 136

6. L. Kohlberg, C. Levine, and A. Hewer, *Moral States: A Current Formulation and a Response to Critics*, pp. 138-139

7. See Owen Flanagan and Kathryn Jackson, "Justice, Care, and Gender: The Kohlberg-Gilligan Debate Revisited."

8. Lawrence Kohlberg, "Education for Justice: A Modern Statement of the Socratic View," in *The Philosophy of Moral Development*, p. 35

9. Lawrence Kohlberg, "Stages of Moral Development as a Basis for Moral Education," in C. M. Beck, et al., *Moral Education*, p. 75

10. Charles Taylor, "The Diversity of Goods," in *Philosophy and the Human Sciences*, p. 234

11. Michael Sandel, *Liberalism and the Limits of Justice*, p. 179

12. Ibid., pp. 133, 177

13. Stuart Hampshire, *Morality and Conflict*, p. 166

14. Alasdair MacIntyre, *After Virtue*, pp. 204-205

15. Hampshire, *Morality and Conflict*, p. 8. Compare MacIntyre, *After Virtue*, p. 119.

16. Roger Scruton, *The Meaning of Conservatism*, p. 21

17. Hampshire, *Morality and Conflict*, pp. 141, 159

18. Ibid., p. 152

19. Hampshire, *Morality and Conflict*, p. 136

20. Ibid.

21. Michael Oakeshott, *Rationalism in Politics*, pp. 1, 61-70

22. Cf. Wittgenstein, *On Certainty*, section 95.

23. Oakeshott, *Rationalism in Politics*, p. 105

24. Hampshire, *Morality and Conflict*, p. 132

25. Ibid., p. 136

26. Edmund Burke, *Reflections on the Revolution in France*, p. 118. Cf. Scruton, *The Meaning of Conservatism*, p. 49.

27. MacIntyre, *After Virtue*, pp. 65-67

28. Bernard Williams, *Ethics and the Limits of Philosophy*, pp. 193-194

29. See John Rawls, "Justice As Fairness: Political Not Metaphysical."

30. Taylor, "The Diversity of Goods," in *Philosophy and the Human Sciences*, p. 238

31. Cf. Annette Baier, "Theory and Reflective Practices," in *Postures of the Mind*, pp. 219-220.

32. Cf. Charles E. Larmore, *Patterns of Moral Complexity*, pp. 5-9.

33. Martha Nussbaum, *The Fragility of Goodness*, pp. 10-11

34. Cf. Ronald Beiner, *Political Judgment*, pp. 103, 178.

35. Richard Rorty, "Postmodernist Bourgeois Liberalism," p. 584; Annette Baier, "Doing Without Moral Theory?," in *Postures of the Mind*, p. 232.

36. Baier, "Doing Without Moral Theory," *Postures of the Mind*, p. 235

37. Hampshire, *Morality and Conflict*, p. 115

38. Cf. W.B. Gallie, "Art as an Essentially Contested Concept," p. 114.

39. MacIntyre, *After Virtue*, p. 206

40. Ibid., p. 115

41. Compare Wittgenstein, *On Certainty*, section 155.

42. These expressions are used repectively by John Kekes, "Moral Conventionalism"; Don Herzog, *Without Foundations: Justification in Political Theory*; Jeffrey Stout, *Ethics After Babel: The Languages of Morals and Their Discontents*.

43. For elaboration of this point see Joshua Cohen's review of Walzer's *Spheres of Justice*.

44. R.H. Tawney, *Commonplace Book*, p. 14

45. Contrast Amy Guttman, "Communitarian Critics of Liberalism." This article is a useful survey of these critics, but it tacitly accepts their frequent conflation of "liberal theory" and "liberal politics."

46. Burke, *Reflections on the Revolution in France*, pp. 106, 120

47. Hans-Georg Gadamer, "The Problem of Historical Consciousness," in P. Rabinow and W. Sullivan, *Interpretative Social Science*, p. 108

48. Rorty, *Philosophy and the Mirror of Nature*, p. 377

49. Richard Rorty, "Solidarity or Objectivity?," in J. Rajchman and C. West, *Post-Analytic Philosophy*, p. 10

50. Rorty, *Philosophy and the Mirror of Nature*, p. 377

51. Louis Raths, et al., *Values and Teaching*, p. 11

52. Kohlberg, et al., *Moral Stages*, pp. 76-78; and Lawrence Kohlberg, "From Is to Ought," in his *The Philosophy of Moral Development*, pp. 169-170

53. Kohlberg, "Stages of Moral Development," in C.M. Beck, et al., *Moral Education*, p. 75

54. For an argument identifying traits of character with virtues and vices (in contrast with the tastes and quirks which define temperament and personality) see N.J.H. Dent, *The Moral Psychology of the Virtues*, p. 10.

55. Kohlberg, "Education for Justice," in *The Philosophy of Moral Development*, p. 35

56. Ibid.

57. Kohlberg, "Stages of Moral Development," in C.M. Beck, et al., *Moral Education*, p. 71

58. Lawrence Kohlberg, "Development as the Aim of Education: The Dewey View," in *The Philosophy of Moral Development*, p. 74

59. Oakeshott, *Rationalism in Politics*, p. 62

60. C.S. Lewis, *The Abolition of Man or Reflections on Education*, p. 185

61. Ibid., pp. 128, 29, 56

62. Compare Roger Scruton, "Freedom and Custom," in A.P. Griffiths, *Of Liberty*.

63. John Rawls, *A Theory of Justice*, pp. 60-61. Ronald Dworkin similarly emphasizes liberties rather than a right to liberty in *Taking Rights Seriously*, pp. 266-78.

64. Compare Rawls, *A Theory of Justice*, pp. 228-29 and 310.

65. Bernard Crick, "Freedom as Politics," in P. Laslett and W.G. Runciman, *Philosophy, Politics and Society*, Third Series, p. 203

66. Contrast Loren Lomasky, "Personal Projects as the Foundation for Basic Rights," in E.F. Paul, et al., *Human Rights*, pp. 35-55; and Dworkin, *Taking Rights Seriously*, p. 182.

67. Compare Arthur C. Danto, "Constructing an Epistemology of Human Rights: A Pseudo Problem?," in E.F. Paul, et al., *Human Rights*, p. 30.

68. Hampshire, *Morality and Conflict*, p. 136; Michael Walzer, *Spheres of Justice*, p. xv

69. See John Rawls, "Kantian Constructivism in Moral Theory" and "Justice as Fairness, Political not Metaphysical." This clarification was anticipated in various passages of *A Theory of Justice*, for example, in Rawls's treatment of moral education as depending largely upon the institutional requirements of human psychological development, pp. 458-479.

70. Walzer, *Spheres of Justice*, p. 313. See also Rawls on caste systems, *A Theory of Justice*, pp. 547-48.

71. Baier, "Doing Without Moral Theory?," in *Postures of the Mind*, pp. 230-31

72. See Burke, *Reflections on the Revolution in France*, p. 116, where he maintains that a political question "will always be . . . a question . . . of probable consequences rather than of positive rights."

73. Kohlberg, "Stages of Moral Development," in C.M. Beck, et al., p. 71

74. Lawrence Kohlberg, "Educating for a Just Society: An Updated and Revised Statement," in B. Munsey, *Moral Development, Moral Education and Kohlberg*, pp. 459 and 466

75. Oakeshott, *Rationalism in Politics*, pp. 107 and 129

76. Kohlberg, "Educating for a Just Society," in Munsey, *Moral Development*, pp. 465-66

77. Lawrence Kohlberg, "The Cognitive-Developmental Approach to Moral Education," in D. Purpel and K. Ryan, *Moral Education*, p. 194. For a different assessment of "what

Kohlberg has been doing all along," see Robert C. Carter, *Dimensions of Moral Education*, pp. 69-70.

78. Kohlberg appears to acknowledge this in "Cognitive-Developmental Theory and the Practice of Collective Moral Education," in M. Wolins and M. Gottesman, *Group Care: An Israeli Approach*, where he notes that "kibbutz youth group practice seems better than anything we can derive from our theory."

79. Cf. Jeffrey Stout, "Virtue Among the Ruins," p. 271.

Chapter 2

1. Ronald Dworkin, "Liberalism," in Stuart Hampshire, *Public and Private Morality*, p. 127

2. See John Rawls, *A Theory of Justice*, pp. 13-14.

3. On the notion of neutrality and its limits see P.J. Crittenden, "Neutrality in Education," p. 8, and R.S. Peters, *John Dewey Reconsidered*, p. 110.

4. J.-J. Rousseau, *Emile*, pp. 197, 66

5. Ibid., p. 54

6. Ibid., p. 55

7. Ibid., pp. 130, 165, 170, 156

8. Ibid., pp. 183-84, 196

9. Ibid., pp. 206, 303, 305

10. Ibid., pp. 292-93

11. Ibid., p. 328

12. Ibid.

13. Ibid., p. 345

14. Ibid., pp. 419, 422, 437

15. Ibid., p. 176

16. Ibid., p. 437

17. Lawrence Kohlberg, "From Is to Ought," in *The Philosophy of Moral Development*, p. 169

18. See Martin L. Hoffman, "Empathy, Its Development and Prosocial Implications," in C.B. Keasey, *Nebraska Symposium on Motivation*, pp. 181-186.

19. Some versions of this view: William Lyons, *Emotion*, pp. 78-79; Charles Taylor, "Explaining Action," pp. 67-71; Gregory Vlastos, "Justice and Equality," in R.B. Brandt, *Social Justice*, pp. 43-45.

20. J.-J. Rousseau, *The First and Second Discourses*, pp. 134-135

21. Aristotle, *Metaphysica*, 982^b19-28

22. Friedrich Nietzsche, *The Gay Science*, section 355

23. Rawls, *A Theory of Justice*, p. 62

24. Hampshire, *Morality and Conflict*, p. 116

25. MacIntyre, *After Conflict*, pp. 160, 206

26. Hampshire, *Morality and Conflict*, p. 160

27. Hampshire, pp. 33, 119

28. Charles Fried, *Right and Wrong*, p. 118

29. Michael Walzer, *Spheres of Justice*, p. xv

30. Alan Gewirth, *Reason and Morality*, pp. 63-64

31. MacIntyre, *After Virtue*, pp. 64-65. Among the others: E.M. Adams, "Gewirth on Reason and Morality," pp. 583-584, and Williams, *Ethics and the Limits of Philosophy*, pp. 58-62.

32. Aristotle, *Nicomachean Ethics*, p. 38

33. Roger Scruton, "Emotion, Practical Knowledge, and Common Culture," in A. Rorty, *Explaining Emotions*, p. 530

34. See Philippa Foot, *Virtues and Vices*, pp. 146-47, and David Wiggins, "Truth, Invention and the Meaning of Life," p. 375.

35. Burke, *Reflections on the Revolution in France*, p. 175

36. See Lewis, *The Abolition of Man* on first principles and Kathleen Gow, *Yes Virginia, There is Right and Wrong!* on core moral precepts.

37. See Alasdair MacIntyre, *A Short History of Ethics*, p. 268, and *After Virtue*, pp. 244-45.

38. This kind of account is pursued by Robert C. Solomon, *The Passions*, pp. 172-213.

39. Williams, *Ethics and the Limits of Philosophy*, pp. 142-148

40. J.S. Mill, *On Liberty*, pp. 19, 34, 47. Compare Aristotle, *Politics*, pp. 146-47.

41. Thus C.B. Macpherson, rejecting this conception of democracy in *The Life and Times of Liberal Democracy*, p. 79.

Chapter 3

1. Martha Nussbaum, "'Finely Aware and Richly Responsible': Moral Attention and the Moral Task of Literature," p. 521

2. Martha C. Nussbaum, *The Fragility of Goodness*, p. 45

3. William James, *Varieties of Religious Experience*, p. 128

4. Ronald de Sousa, "The Rationality of Emotions," in A. Rorty, *Explaining Emotions*, pp. 136-137. The point is developed in de Sousa's *The Rationality of Emotion*, pp. 195-196 and following.

5. John McDowell, "Virtue and Reason," p. 345

6. Sabina Lovibond, *Realism and Imagination in Ethics*, p. 22

7. McDowell, "Virtue and Reason," p. 346

8. Cora Diamond, "Anything but Argument?," pp. 31, 37-37

9. Ibid., p. 34

10. Lawrence Kohlberg, *The Philosophy of Moral Development*, p. 398

11. George Grant, *Lament for a Nation*, p. 79

12. Roberto Unger, *Knowledge and Politics*, p. 39. See also Charles C. Anderson and L.C. Travis, *Psychology and the Liberal Consensus*, pp. 48, 124.

13. See James D. Wallace, *Virtues and Vices*, pp. 18-25.

14. Lawrence Kohlberg, "Stages of Moral Development as a Basis for Moral Education," in C. Beck, et al., *Moral Education, p. 75*

15. Thomas Szasz, *Ideology and Insanity*, p. 210

16. *Ibid.*, p. 50

17. See Hugh Hartshorne and M.A. May, *Studies in the Nature of Character*, and J. Phillipe Rushton, *Altruism, Socialization, and Society*, pp. 63-64.

18. Cf. Max Horkheimer, *Eclipse of Reason*, Herbert Marcuse, *One-Dimensional Man*, Jürgen Habermas, *Legitimation Crisis*, and Leo Strauss, *Natural Right and History*.

19. John Macmurray, *Reason and Emotion*, p. 15

20. John Dewey, *Theory of Valuation*, p. 30

21. *Ibid.*, p. 26

22. John Dewey, *Experience and Nature*, pp. 299-300

23. John Dewey, *Art as Experience*, p. 30

24. Richard Rorty, "The Priority of Democracy to Philosophy," footnote 33, in M. Peterson and R. Vaughan, *The Virginia Statute of Religious Freedom*

25. Max Scheler, *Formalism in Ethics and Non-Formal Ethics of Values*, p. 253. Scheler holds this to be "a prejudice that has its historical origin in antiquity."

26. Martin Heidegger, *Being and Time*, p. 180. Cf. p. 390.

27. Richard Rorty, *Philosophy and the Mirror of Nature*, p. 5

28. Contrast R.S. Peters, *John Dewey Reconsidered*, and Salvatore D'urso, "Can Dewey Be Marx's Educational-Philosophical Representative?"

29. Richard Brandt, *A Theory of the Good and the Right*, p. 94

30. Ibid., p. 113

31. Ibid., pp. 138-148

32. Ibid., p. 94

33. Jerome A. Shaffer, "An Assessment of Emotion," p. 164

34. Ibid., p. 169

35. Scheler, *Formalism in Ethics*, p. 264

36. Ibid., p. 254

37. McDowell, "Virtue and Reason," p. 346

38. Heidegger, *Being and Time*, p. 392

39. This case is elaborated in Evan Simpson, *Reason over Passion*, pp. 29-35. See also Stanley G. Clarke, "Emotions: Rationality without Cognitivism."

40. See Stephen Leighton, "Feelings and Emotions," p. 308.

41. Leslie A. Marchand, *Byron, A Biography*, p. 33

42. See Patricia S. Greenspan, "Emotions as Evaluations," pp. 162-165.

43. R.B. Zajonc, "On the Primacy of Affect," in K.R. Scherer and P. Ekman, *Approaches to Emotion*

44. This case is elaborated in Clarke, "Emotions: Rationality Without Cognitivism."

45. Leighton, "Feelings and Emotion," p. 308

46. Cf. Norton Nelkin, "Pains and Pain Sensations," p. 143.

47. Paul Ekman, "Biological and Cultural Contributions to Bodily and Facial Movement in the Expression of Emotions," in A. Rorty, ed., *Explaining Emotions*, pp. 80-84

48. See Jenefer Robinson, "Emotion, Judgment, and Desire," pp. 731-741.

49. Bernard Williams, *Ethics and the Limits of Philosophy*, p. 149

50. Ibid., pp. 149-151

51. Taylor and Rorty exchange these views in their respective articles, "Understanding in Human Science" and "A Reply to Dreyfus and Taylor."

52. Diamond, "Anything but Argument?," p. 31

53. Annette Baier, "Doing Without Moral Theory?," in *Postures of the Mind*, p. 238

54. Williams, *Ethics and the Limits of Philosophy*, p. 153

55. Hans-Georg Gadamer, *Philosophical Hermeneutics*, p. 9

56. Lovibond, *Realism and Imagination in Ethics*, p. 121

57. Cf. Wittgenstein, *On Certainty*, section 422.

58. Paulo Freire, *Pedagogy of the Oppressed*, pp. 91, 181, 184-185

59. George Grant, *Lament for a Nation*, p. 96

60. Ibid., p. 94

61. Alasdair MacIntyre, *After Virtue*, pp. 6-10

62. Ibid., 2nd ed., p. 276

63. W.V Quine, *Word and Object*, p. 4

64. L. Kohlberg, C. Levine, and A. Hewer, *Moral Stages: A Current Formulation and a Response to Critics*, p. 164

Chapter 4

1. See Louis Raths, et al., *Values and Teaching*, pp. 11, 286, 296. References are to the 2nd edition except where noted.

2. John Dewey, *Reconstruction in Philosophy*, pp. 162-63

3. Raths, *Values and Teaching*, p. 34

4. Ibid., pp. 22, 42

5. Ibid., p. 22

6. Ibid., p. 41-42

7. See Lawrence Kohlberg, "Education for Justice: A Modern Statement of the Socratic View" and "From *Is* to *Ought*: How to Commit the Naturalistic Fallacy and Get Away with It in the Study of Moral Philosophy," in *The Philosophy of Moral Development*, pp. 31-35 and 183-84.

8. See, e.g., Urie Bronfenbrenner, *Two Worlds of Childhood*, p. 77; Alan L. Lockwood, "A Critical View of Values Clarification," in D. Purpel and K. Ryan, *Moral Education*, p.

158; and George Bereday, et al., *The Changing Soviet School*, p. 422.

9. Raths, *Values and Teaching*, pp. 27-28

10. See Howard Kirschenbaum, "Beyond Values Clarification," in H. Kirschenbaum and S. Simon, *Readings in Values Clarification*, pp. 95-99.

11. See, for example, Hugh Nevin, "Values Clarification: Perspectives in John Dewey with Implications for Religious Education," pp. 670-71; John S. Stewart, "Problems and Contradictions of Values Clarification," in Purpel and Ryan, *Moral Education*, pp. 127-38; and Arvid W. Adell, "Values Clarification Revisited," in Wesley Cragg, *Contemporary Moral Issues*, pp. 522-23.

12. Raths, *Values and Teaching*, p. 26

13. For various examples of these techniques see part 3 of both editions of Raths, *Values and Teaching*; S. Simon, et al., *Values Clarification: A Handbook of Practical Strategies for Teachers and Students*; and M. Harmin, et al., *Clarifying Values through Subject Matter*.

14. John Dewey, *The Quest for Certainty*, p. 258. Compare Nevin, "Values Clarification: Perspectives in John Dewey," pp. 670-71.

15. Dewey, *The Quest for Certainty*, p. 260. Compare George J. Harrison, "Values Clarification and the Construction of the Good," p. 187.

16. Dewey, *The Quest for Certainty*, p. 264

17. See Raths, *Values and Teaching*, p. 7.

18. Ibid., pp. 272-75

19. See John L. Harrison, "Values Clarification: an Appraisal," p. 27.

20. See Raths, *Values and Teaching*, 1st ed., pp. 197-200.

21. See Lockwood, "A Critical View of Values Clarification," in Purpel and Ryan, *Moral Education*, p. 159.

22. See Kathleen Gow, *Yes Virginia, There is Right and Wrong!*, p. 172.

23. R.M. Hare, *Freedom and Reason*, p. 172

24. Raths, *Values and Teaching*, p. 299

25. Abraham H. Maslow, *Motivation and Personality*, p. 22. For an application of such views to the classroom, see Louis E. Raths and Anna E. Purrell, *Understanding the Problem Child*.

26. See James S. Leming, "Curricular Effectiveness in Moral/Values Education," pp. 150-51; and Alan L. Lockwood, "The Effects of Values Clarification and Moral Development Curricula on School-Age Subjects," p. 344.

27. Howard Kirschenbaum, "Clarifying Values Clarification," in Purpel and Ryan, *Moral Education*, p. 122

28. Milton Rokeach, "Towards a Philosophy of Value Education," in John Meyer, et al., *Values Education*, p. 123

29. See R.S. Peters, *John Dewey Reconsidered*, p. 110.

30. H.H. Price, "Clarity Is Not Enough," in H.D. Lewis, ed., *Clarity Is Not Enough*, pp. 16-17

31. Ibid., p. 24

32. Lawrence Kohlberg, "The Relationship of Moral Education to the Broader Field of Values Education," in Meyer, et al., *Values Education*, p. 80

33. Ibid.

34. Raths, *Values and Teaching*, pp. 145-47, 296-297

35. John Dewey, *How We Think*, pp. 83, 88

36. Oakeshott, *Rationalism in Politics*, p. 68

37. Kohlberg, "From *Is* to *Ought*," in *The Philosophy of Moral Development*, pp. 132, 136-37

38. See J.R. Rest, *Development in Judging Moral Issues.*

39. See, among his other writings, Lawrence Kohlberg, "The Child as a Moral Philosopher," "Education for Justice," and "Justice as Reversibility." The latter two pieces are included in *The Philosophy of Moral Development.*

40. Rousseau, *Emile*, pp. 197, 53, 66

41. Ibid, p. 197

42. Ibid, p. 70

43. Kohlberg, "Indoctrination Versus Relativity in Value Education," in *The Philosophy of Moral Development*, p. 17

44. Ibid., pp. 17, 148

45. Ibid., p. 18

46. Ibid., p. 150

47. Ibid., pp. 18, 150-151

48. Ibid., p. 18

49. Lawrence Kohlberg, Foreword to Rest, *Development in Judging Moral Issues*, p. ix; and Lawrence Kohlberg, "Educating for a Just Society: An Updated and Revised Statement," in B. Munsey, *Moral Development*, p. 457

50. Kohlberg, "From *Is* to *Ought*," in *The Philosophy of Moral Development*, p. 101-102

51. Ibid., p. 137

52. For a review of the empirical basis of Kohlberg's theory see Martin L. Hoffman, "Moral Development," in H. Mussen, *Carmichael's Manual of Psychology*, Vol. 2, pp. 278-282.

53. See Norman Williams and Sheila Williams, *The Moral Development of Children*, p. 80, and Lawrence Kohlberg, "The Child as a Moral Philosopher," p. 28.

54. See E. L. Simpson, "Moral Development Research: A Case of Scientific Cultural Bias," p. 92. For a more general examination of Kohlberg's supposed ideological bias see E. V. Sullivan, *Kohlberg's Structuralism*.

55. Cf. Robert Selman, "Toward a Structural Analysis of Developing Interpersonal Relations Concepts," in A.D. Pick, *Minnesota Symposia on Child Psychology*, vol. 10.

56. Compare R. S. Peters, *Reason and Compassion*, p. 104.

57. Kohlberg, "From *Is* to *Ought*," in *The Philosophy of Moral Development*, pp. 139-141

58. Ibid., pp. 55, 58

59. J.P. Rushton, "Altruism and Society," pp. 436-440

60. Compare Justin Aronfreed, *Conduct and Conscience*, pp. 242-43.

61. Cf. S. Milgram, "Behavioral Study of Obedience."

62. Kohlberg, "Development as the Aim of Education: The Dewey View," in *The Philosophy of Moral Development*, pp. 51, 54

63. See W. Alston, "Comments on Kohlberg's 'From Is to Ought,'" in T. Mischel, *Cognitive Development and Epistemology*, pp. 278-280; and Robert E. Carter, *Dimensions of Moral Education*, pp. 96-105, where he makes the suggestion that, having left emotions out of his six-stage structure, Kohlberg then tacks them onto a supposed "Stage 7."

64. Kohlberg, "From *Is* to *Ought*," in *The Philosophy of Moral Development*, p. 134

65. L. Kohlberg, "Stages of Moral Development," in Beck, et al., *Moral Education*, p. 46

66. Rousseau, *Emile*, p. 293

67. Bill Puka, "An Interdisciplinary Treatment of Kohlberg," p. 476

68. See Elliot Turiel, "Distinct Conceptual and Developmental Domains: Social Convention and Morality," in C. Keasey, *Nebraska Symposium on Motivation*. See also Larry P. Nucci, "Conceptual Development in the Moral and Conventional Domains."

69. See David Gautier's comments in Beck, et al., *Moral Education*, pp. 365-66.

70. L. Kohlberg, "Moral Stages and Moralization," in T. Lickona, *Moral Development and Behavior*, p. 35

71. L. Kohlberg and R. Kramer, "Continuities and Discontinuities in Childhood and Adult Moral Development," p. 118; L. Kohlberg, "Continuities in Childhood and Adulthood Moral Development Revisited," in P. Baltes and K. Schaie, *Life-Span Developmental Psychology*, p. 180

72. John C. Gibbs, "Kohlberg's Moral Stage Theory: A Piagetian Revision," pp. 89-112

73. Compare John Rawls, *A Theory of Justice*, p. 462n.

74. See Kohlberg, "Stages of Moral Development," in C. Beck, et al., *Moral Education*, pp. 90-92.

75. Ibid., p. 60

76. Ibid., pp. 60-61

77. Kohlberg, "Education for Justice," in *The Philosophy of Moral Development*, p. 39

78. Ibid., p. 167-168

79. Kohlberg, "The Cognitive-Developmental Approach to Moral Education," in Purpel and Ryan, *Moral Education*, p. 184

80. Gilligan, *In a Different Voice*, p. 73

81. Cf. Larmore, *Patterns of Moral Complexity*, p. 5-6.

82. Rousseau, *Emile*, pp. 141, 57

83. Kohlberg, "Stages of Moral Development," in C. Beck, et al., *Moral Education*, p. 71

84. Rousseau, *Emile*, p. 288

85. Kohlberg, "Stages of Moral Development," in C. Beck, et al., *Moral Education*, p. 78

86. See Alan L. Lockwood, "The Effects of Values Clarification and Moral Development Curricula on School-Age Subjects," p. 358.

87. See J. S. Mill, *Considerations on Representative Government*, pp. 411-12, 534-45.

88. M. Oakeshott, *Rationalism in Politics*, p. 68

89. L. Kohlberg, "The Child as a Moral Philosopher," p. 30. See also "Stages of Moral Development," in C. Beck, et al., *Moral Education*, p. 36.

Chapter 5

1. L.S. Vygotsky, *Mind in Society*, p. 122

2. Ibid., pp. 79-80. Compare R.S. Peters, *Reason and Compassion*, p. 69.

3. L.S. Vygotsky, *Mind and Society*, p. 88

4. Jean Piaget, *The Moral Judgment of the Child*, pp. 104-105

5. R.S. Peters, *Psychology and Ethical Development*, p. 349

Notes

6. Israel Scheffler, "The Moral Content of American Public Education," in Purpel and Ryan, *Moral Education*, pp. 22-23

7. Cf. Susan Buck-Morss, "Socio-economic Bias in Piaget's Theory," and H. Reid and E.J. Yanarella, "Critical Political Theory and Moral Development." Contrast James Youniss, "Beyond Ideology to the Universals of Development."

8. Cf. James Rest, *Development in Judging Moral Issues*.

9. James Youniss, "Dialectical Theory and Piaget on Social Knowledge," p. 235

10. Cora Diamond, "Anything but Argument?," p. 32

11. Martha C. Nussbaum, *The Fragility of Goodness*, p. 14

12. Larmore, *Patterns of Moral Complexity*, pp. 40-41

13. Cf. R.M. Henry, *The Psychodynamic Foundations of Morality*. See also J.P. Rushton, "Altruism and Society," pp. 440-41, and Elizabeth L. Simpson, "A Holistic Approach to Moral Development and Behavior," in T. Lickona, *Moral Development and Behavior*.

14. See Evan Simpson, "The Subjects of Justice," pp. 490-491.

15. See Franz de Waal, *Chimpanzee Politics: Power and Sex Among Apes*.

16. Hobbes, *Leviathan*, p. 116

17. Kohlberg, "From *Is* to *Ought*," in *The Philosophy of Moral Development*, pp. 155, 166-167

18. Ibid., pp. 153-154, 167

19. Lawrence Kohlberg, "Educating for Justice: an Updated and Revised Statement," in Munsey, *Moral Development, Moral Education and Kohlberg*, p. 457

20. R.J. Burke, "Politics as Rhetoric," p. 54

21. Edmund Burke, *Reflections on the Revolution in France*, pp. 194-195

22. L. Kohlberg, et al., *Moral Stages*, pp. 44-46

23. Cf. N. Emler, et al., "The Relationship between Moral Reasoning and Political Orientation."

24. See L. Kohlberg and R. Kramer, "Continuities and Discontinuities in Childhood and Adult Moral Development"; and L. Kohlberg, "Continuities in Childhood and Adult Moral Development Revisited," in P. Baltes and K. Schaie, *Life Span Developmental Psychology*.

25. L. Kohlberg, "Stage and Sequence: the Cognitive-Developmental Approach to Socialization," in D. Goslin, *Handbook of Socialization Theory and Research*, p. 385

26. Lawrence Kohlberg, "The Future of Liberalism as the Dominant Ideology of the Western World," in *The Philosophy of Moral Development*, p. 239

27. Jürgen Habermas, *Communication and the Evolution of Society*, p. 90

28. On Piaget's view see M. Chapman, "The Structure of Exchange"; on Habermas's see his "Reply to My Critics," in Thompson and Held, *Habermas: Critical Debates*, p. 260.

29. Jürgen Habermas, *Theory and Practice*, pp. 25-26

30. Kohlberg, et al., *Moral Stages*, p. 164

31. The growing body of literature on relationships between communication and moral development includes Thomas McCarthy, *The Critical Theory of Jürgen Habermas*. For additional references see John M. Broughton, "Cognitive Interaction and the Development of Sociality."

32. Habermas, *Communication and the Evolution of Society*, p. 122

33. Oakeshott, *Rationalism in Politics*, p. 70

34. Hampshire, *Morality and Conflict*, p. 164

35. Lovibond, *Realism and Imagination in Ethics*, p. 216

36. See Ronald Dworkin, *Law's Empire*, Ch. 1. For criticisms, explicit or implied, and some interesting disanalogies between law and literature, see the pieces by MacCormick, Bickenbach, and Shiner in E. Simpson, *Anti-Foundationalism and Practical Reasoning*.

37. Cf. George Woodcock's view of Orwell's moral politics, *The Crystal Palace*, p. 282.

38. Bernstein, *Philosophical Profiles*, pp. 109, 114

Conclusion

1. Cf. Frank Sibley's still-valuable "Aesthetic Concepts," in C. Barrett, *Collected Papers on Aesthetics*. Sibley notes a pattern of development in aesthetic appreciation, ranging from egoistic delight or aversion expressed in a basic vocabulary of "pretty" and "ugly" to admiration and contempt

expressed in distinctions like "gay" and "garish," "rich" and "ostentatious."

2. See W.E. Kennick, "Does Traditional Aesthetics Rest on a Mistake?," in C. Barrett, *Collected Papers on Aesthetics*. See also the interesting essay by H.A. Prichard, "Does Moral Philosophy Rest on a Mistake?," in *Moral Obligation*.

3. Cf. Lawrence Kohlberg, "Moral Psychology and the Theory of Tragedy," in *The Philosophy of Moral Development*, and F. Clark Power and Lawrence Kohlberg, "Religion, Morality, and Ego Development," in J. Fowler and A. Vergote, *Toward Moral and Religious Maturity*. See also Part V of J. M. Broughton and D. John Freeman-Moir, *The Cognitive-Developmental Psychology of John Mark Baldwin*, where Baldwin's interest in religious and aesthetic development is described in terms of "the Piagetian-Kohlbergian tradition."

4. Power and Kohlberg, "Religion, Morality and Ego Development," p. 364, and Kohlberg, "Continuities in Childhood and Adult Moral Development Revisited," p. 203

Bibliography

Adams, E.M., "Gewirth on Reason and Morality," *Review of Metaphysics* 33 (1980) 579-592

Anderson, Charles C., and L.C. Travis, *Psychology and the Liberal Consensus* (Waterloo, Ont.: Wilfrid Laurier University Press 1983)

Aristotle, *Metaphysica* (Oxford: Clarendon Press, 2nd ed. 1972)

Aristotle, *Nicomachean Ethics* (London: Oxford University Press 1961)

Aristotle, *Politics* (Oxford: Clarendon Press 1960)

Aronfreed, Justin, *Conduct and Conscience: The Socialization of Internalized Control over Behavior* (New York: Academic Press 1968)

Baier, Annette, *Postures of the Mind: Essays on Mind and Morals* (London: Methuen 1985)

Baltes, P.B., and K.W. Schaie, eds., *Life-Span Developmental Psychology: Research and Theory* (New York: Academic Press 1973)

Barrett, Cyril, ed., *Collected Papers on Aesthetics* (Oxford: Blackwell 1965)

Beck, C.M., B.S. Crittenden, and E.V. Sullivan, eds., *Moral Education: Interdisciplinary Approaches* (New York: Newman Press 1971)

Beiner, Ronald, *Political Judgment* (London: Methuen 1983)

Bereday, George, William W. Brickman, and Gerald H. Read, eds., *The Changing Soviet School* (Boston: Houghton Mifflin 1960)

Bernstein, Richard, *Philosophical Profiles* (Philadelphia: University of Pennsylvania Press 1986)

Boyd, Dwight, "The Moralberry Pie: Some Basic Concepts," *Theory into Practice* 16 (1977) 67-72

Boyd, Dwight, and Lawrence Kohlberg, "The Is-Ought Problem: A Developmental Perspective," *Zygon* 8 (1973) 358-372

Brandt, R.B., ed., *Social Justice* (Englewood Cliffs, NJ: Prentice-Hall 1962)

Brandt, R.B., *A Theory of the Good and the Right* (Oxford: Clarendon Press 1979)

Bronfenbrenner, Urie, *Two Worlds of Childhood* (New York: Russell Sage Foundation 1970)

Broughton, John M., "Cognitive Interaction and the Development of Sociality: A Commentary on Damon and Killen," *Merrill-Palmer Quarterly* 28 (1982) 369-378

Broughton, John M., and D.J. Freeman-Moir, eds., *The CognitiveDevelopmental Psychology of James Mark Baldwin: Current Theory and Research in Genetic Epistemology* (Norwood, NJ: ABLEX Publishing 1982)

Buck-Morss, Susan, "Socio-economic Bias in Piaget's Theory and Its Implications for Cross-culture Studies," *Human Development* 18 (1975) 35-49

Burke, Edmund, *Reflections on the Revolution in France* (1790) (Harmondsworth: Middlesex 1968)

Burke, Richard J., "Politics as Rhetoric," *Ethics* 93 (1982) 45-55

Bibliography

Carter, Robert E., *Dimensions of Moral Education* (Toronto: University of Toronto Press 1984)

Clarke, Stanley G., "Emotions: Rationality without Cognitivism," *Dialogue: Canadian Philosophical Review* 25 (1986) 663-674

Clarke, Stanley G., and Evan Simpson, eds., *Anti-Theory in Ethics and Moral Conservatism* (Albany: SUNY Press 1989)

Chapman, M., "The Structure of Exchange: Piaget's Sociological Theory," *Human Development* 29 (1986) 181-194

Cohen, Joshua, review of Walzer's *Spheres of Justice, Journal of Philosophy* 83 (1986) 457-468

Cragg, Wesley, ed., *Contemporary Moral Issues* (Toronto: McGraw Hill-Ryerson 1983)

Crittenden, P.J., "Neutrality in Education (Reflections on a Paulo Freire Thesis)," *Educational Philosophy and Theory* 12, No. 1 (June 1980) 1-18

Dent, N.J.H., *The Moral Psychology of the Virtues* (Cambridge: Cambridge University Press 1984)

de Sousa, Ronald, *The Rationality of Emotion* (Cambridge, MA: MIT Press 1987)

de Waal, Franz, *Chimpanzee Politics: Power and Sex Among Apes* (London: Jonathan Cape 1982)

Dewey, John, *Art as Experience* (New York: Minton, Balch and Co. 1934)

Dewey, John, *Experience and Nature* (Chicago: Open Court 1925)

Dewey, John, *How We Think: A Restatement of the Relation of Reflective Thinking to the Educative Process* (Boston: D.C. Heath and Co. 1933)

Dewey, John, *The Quest for Certainty* (New York: Minton, Balch and Co. 1929)

Dewey, John, *Reconstruction in Philosophy* (New York: Henry Holt 1920)

Dewey, John, *Theory of Valuation* (Chicago: University of Chicago Press 1939)

Diamond, Cora, "Anything But Argument?," *Philosophical Investigations* 5 (1982) 23-41

D'urso, Salvatore, "Can Dewey Be Marx's Educational-Philosophical Representative?," *Educational Philosophy and Theory* 12, No. 2 (October 1980) 21-35

Dworkin, Ronald, *Law's Empire* (Cambridge, MA: Harvard University Press 1986)

Dworkin, Ronald, *Taking Rights Seriously* (Cambridge, MA: Harvard University Press 1977)

Empson, William, *Collected Poems* (London: Chatto and Windus 1955)

Ember, N., S. Renwick, and B. Malone, "The Relationship Between Moral Reasoning and Political Orientation," *Journal of Personality and Social Psychology* 34 (1983) 1073-1080

Foot, Philippa, *Virtues and Vices and Other Essays in Moral Philosophy* (Berkeley: University of California Press 1978)

Flanagan, Owen, and Kathryn Jackson, "Justice, Care, and Gender: The Kohlberg-Gilligan Debate Revisited," *Ethics* 97 (1987) 622-637

Fowler, J.W., and A. Vergote, eds., *Toward Moral and Religious Maturity* (Morristown, NJ: Silver Burdett 1980)

212

Bibliography

Freire, Paulo, *Pedagogy of the Oppressed* (New York: Seabury Press 1970)

Fried, Charles, *Right and Wrong* (Cambridge, MA: Harvard University Press 1978)

Gadamer, Hans-Georg, *Philosophical Hermeneutics* (Berkeley: University of California Press 1976)

Gibbs, John C., "Kohlberg's Moral Stage Theory: A Piagetian Revision," *Human Development* 22 (1979) 89-112

Gallie, W.B., "Art as an Essentially Contested Concept," *Philosophical Quarterly* 6 (1956) 97-114

Gilligan, Carol, *In a Different Voice: Psychological Theory and Woman's Development* (Cambridge, MA: Harvard University Press 1982)

Goslin, D.A., ed., *Handbook of Socialization Theory and Research* (New York: Rand-McNally 1969)

Gow, Kathleen M., *Yes Virginia, There Is Right and Wrong!* (Toronto: John Wiley and Sons 1980)

Grant, George, *Lament for a Nation: The Defeat of Canadian Nationalism* (Toronto: McClelland and Stewart 1970)

Greenspan, Patricia S., "Emotions as Evaluations," *Pacific Philosophical Quarterly* 62 (1981) 158-169

Griffiths, A.P., ed., *Of Liberty* (Cambridge: Cambridge University Press 1983)

Guttman, Amy, "Communitarian Critics of Liberalism," *Philosophy and Public Affairs* 14 (1985) 308-322

Habermas, Jürgen, *Communication and the Evolution of Society* (Boston: Beacon Press 1979)

Habermas, Jürgen, *Legitimation Crisis* (Boston: Beacon Press 1975)

Habermas, Jürgen, *Theory and Practice* (Boston: Beacon Press 1973)

Hampshire, Stuart, *Morality and Conflict* (Cambridge, MA: Harvard University Press 1983)

Hampshire, Stuart, ed., *Public and Private Morality* (Cambridge: Cambridge University Press 1978)

Hare, R.M., *Freedom and Reason* (Oxford: Clarendon Press 1963)

Harmin, Merrill, Howard Kirschenbaum, and Sidney B. Simon, eds., *Clarifying Values through Subject Matter: Applications for the Classroom* (Minneapolis: Winston Press 1973)

Harrison, George J., "Values Clarification and the Construction of Good," *Educational Theory* 30 (1980) 185-191

Harrison, John L., "Values Clarification: An Appraisal," *Journal of Moral Education* 6 (1976) 22-31

Hartshorne, Hugh, and M.A. May, *Studies in the Nature of Character*, 3 vols. (New York: Macmillan 1928-30)

Hauerwas, S., and A. MacIntyre, eds., *Revisions* (Notre Dame: Notre Dame University Press 1983)

Heidegger, Martin, *Being and Time* (New York: Harper and Row 1962)

Held, Virginia, "Feminism and Epistemology: Recent Work on the Connection between Gender and Knowledge," *Philosophy and Public Affairs* 14 (1985) 296-307

Henry, R.M., *The Psychodynamic Foundations of Morality* (Basil: S. Karger 1983)

Bibliography

Herzog, Don, *Without Foundations: Justification in Political Theory* (Ithaca: Cornell University Press 1985)

Hobbes, Thomas, *Leviathan* (1651) (Oxford: Clarendon Press 1965)

Horkheimer, Max, *Eclipse of Reason* (New York: Seabury Press 1947)

Hume, David, *Enquiries Concerning the Human Understanding and Concerning the Principles of Morals* (1748 and 1751) (Oxford: Clarendon Press, 2nd ed. 1963)

Hume, David, *A Treatise of Human Nature* (1739) (Oxford: Clarendon Press 1960)

James, William, *Varieties of Religious Experience* (New York: Mentor Books 1958)

Keasey, C.B., ed., *Nebraska Symposium on Motivation*, Vol. 25 (Lincoln: University of Nebraska Press 1977)

Kirschenbaum, Howard, and Sidney B. Simon, eds., *Readings in Values Clarification* (Minneapolis: Winston Press 1973)

Kohlberg, Lawrence, "The Child as Moral Philosopher," *Psychology Today* 3 (1968) 25-30

Kohlberg, Lawrence, *The Philosophy of Moral Development* (San Francisco: Harper and Row 1981)

Kohlberg, Lawrence, and R. Kramer, "Continuities and Discontinuities in Childhood and Adult Moral Development," *Human Development* 12 (1969) 92-120

Kohlberg, L., C. Levine, and A. Hewer, *Moral Stages: A Current Formulation and a Response to Critics* (Basil: S. Karger 1983)

Larmore, Charles E., *Patterns of Moral Complexity* (Cambridge: Cambridge University Press 1987)

Laslett, P., and W.G. Runciman, eds., *Philosophy, Politics and Society*, Third Series (Oxford: Blackwell 1967)

Leighton, Stephen, "Feelings and Emotion," *Review of Metaphysics* 38 (1984) 303-320

Leming, James S., "Curricular Effectiveness in Moral/Values Education: A Review of Research," *Journal of Moral Education* 10 (1981) 147-164

Lewis, C.S., *The Abolition of Man or Reflections on Education with Special Reference to the Teaching of English in the Upper Forms of Schools* (New York: Macmillan 1975)

Lewis, H.D., ed., *Clarity Is Not Enough: Essays in Criticism of Linguistic Philosophy* (London: George Allen and Unwin 1963)

Lickona, Thomas, ed., *Moral Development and Behavior: Theory, Research, and Social Issues* (New York: Holt, Rinehart and Winston 1976)

Lockwood, Alan L., "The Effects of Values Clarification and Moral Development Curricula on School-Age Subjects: A Critical Review of Recent Research," *Review of Educational Research* 48 (1978) 325-364

Lovibond, Sabina, *Realism and Imagination in Ethics* (Minneapolis: The University of Minnesota Press 1983)

Lyons, William, *Emotion* (Cambridge: Cambridge University Press 1980)

MacIntyre, Alasdair, *After Virtue, A Study in Moral Theory* (Notre Dame: Notre Dame University Press 1981, 2nd ed. 1984)

MacIntyre, Alasdair, *A Short History of Ethics: A History of Moral Philosophy from the Homeric Age to the Twentieth Century* (London: Routledge and Kegan Paul 1966)

Bibliography

MacMurray, John, *Reason and Emotion* (London: Faber and Faber 1935)

Macpherson, C.B., *The Life and Times of Liberal Democracy* (Oxford: Oxford University Press 1977)

Marchand, Leslie A., *Byron: A Biography* (New York: Alfred A. Knopf 1957)

Marcuse, Herbert, *One Dimensional Man: Studies in the Ideology of Advanced Industrial Society* (London: Routledge and Kegan Paul 1964)

Maslow, Abraham H., *Motivation and Personality* (New York: Harper and Row, 2nd ed. 1970)

McCarthy, Thomas, *The Critical Theory of Jürgen Habermas* (Cambridge, MA: MIT Press 1981)

McDowell, John, "Virtue and Reason," *The Monist* 62 (1979) 331-350

Meyer, John, Brian Burnham, and John Cholvat, eds., *Values Education: Theory/Practice/Problems/Prospects* (Waterloo, Ont.: Wilfrid Laurier University Press 1975)

Milgram, S., "Behavioral Study of Obedience," *Journal of Abnormal and Social Psychology* 67 (1963) 371-378

Mill, J.S., *Considerations on Representative Government*, in the *Collected Works*, vol. 19 (Toronto: University of Toronto Press 1977)

Mill, J.S., *On Liberty* (1859) (Northbrook, IL: AHM Publishing 1947)

Mischel, Theodore, ed., *Cognitive Development and Epistemology* (New York: Academic Press 1971)

Munsey, B., ed., *Moral Development, Moral Education and Kohlberg: Basic Ideas in Philosophy, Psychology, Religion, and Education* (Birmingham, AL: Religious Education Press 1980)

Mussen, P.H., ed., *Carmichael's Manual of Psychology*, vol. 2 (New York: John Wiley and Sons, 3rd ed. 1970)

Nelkin, Norton, "Pains and Pain Sensations," *Journal of Philosophy* 83 (1986) 129-148

Nevin, Hugh, "Values Clarification: Perspectives in John Dewey with Implications for Religious Education," *Religious Education* 73 (1978) 661-677

Nietzsche, Friedrich, *The Gay Science* (1887) (New York: Vintage Books 1974)

Nucci, Larry P., "Conceptual Development in the Moral and Conventional Domains: Implications for Values Education," *Review of Educational Research* 52 (1982) 93-122

Nussbaum, Martha, "'Finely Aware and Richly Responsible': Moral Attention and the Moral Task of Literature," *Journal of Philosophy* 82 (1985) 516-529

Nussbaum, Martha C., *The Fragility of Goodness. Luck and Ethics in Greek Tragedy and Philosophy* (Cambridge: Cambridge University Press 1986)

Oakeshott, Michael, *Rationalism in Politics and Other Essays* (London: Methuen 1974)

Paul, E.F., F.D. Miller, Jr., and J. Paul, eds., *Human Rights* (Oxford: Blackwell 1984)

Peters, R.S., *John Dewey Reconsidered* (London: Routledge and Kegan Paul 1977)

Peters, R.S., *Psychology and Ethical Development* (London: George Allen and Unwin 1974)

Bibliography

Peters, R.S., *Reason and Compassion* (London: Routledge and Kegan Paul 1973)

Peterson, Merrill and R. Vaughan, eds., *The Virginia Statute of Religious Freedom* (Cambridge: Cambridge University Press 1987)

Piaget, Jean, *The Moral Judgment of the Child* (London: Routledge and Kegan Paul 1968)

Pick, A.D., ed., *Minnesota Symposia on Child Psychology*, vol. 10 (Minneapolis: University of Minnesota Press 1976)

Prichard, H.A., *Moral Obligation* (Oxford: Clarendon Press 1949)

Puka, Bill, "An Interdisciplinary Treatment of Kohlberg," *Ethics* 92 (1982) 468-490

Purpel, David, and Kevin Ryan, eds., *Moral Education ... It Comes With the Territory* (Berkeley: McCutchan Publishing Corporation 1976)

Quine, Willard Van Orman, *Word and Object* (Cambridge, MA: MIT Press 1960)

Rabinow, P. and W.M. Sullivan, *Interpretative Social Science: A Reader* (Berkeley: University of California Press 1979)

Rajchman, J., and C. West, eds., *Post-Analytic Philosophy* (New York: Columbia University Press 1985)

Raths, Louis E., and Anna E. Purrell, *Understanding the Problem Child* (Orange, NJ: Economics Press 1962)

Raths, Louis, Merrill Harmin, and Sidney B. Simon, *Values and Teaching. Working with Values in the Classroom* (Columbus: Charles E. Merrill, 1st ed. 1966, 2nd ed. 1978)

Rawls, John, "Justice as Fairness, Political Not Metaphysical," *Philosophy and Public Affairs* 14 (1985) 223-251

Rawls, John, "Kantian Constructivism in Moral Theory," *Journal of Philosophy* 87 (1980) 515-572

Rawls, John, *A Theory of Justice* (Cambridge, MA: Harvard University Press 1971)

Reid, H., and E.J. Yanarella, "Critical Political Theory and Moral Development: On Kohlberg, Hampden-Turner, and Habermas," *Theory and Society* 4 (1977) 505-541

Rest, J.R., *Development in Judging Moral Issues* (Minneapolis: University of Minnesota Press 1979)

Robinson, Jenefer, "Emotion, Judgment, and Desire," *Journal of Philosophy* 80 (1983) 731-41

Rorty, A., ed., *Explaining Emotions* (Berkeley: University of California Press 1980)

Rorty, Richard, *Philosophy and the Mirror of Nature* (Princeton, NJ: Princeton University Press 1979)

Rorty, Richard, "Postmodernist Bourgeois Liberalism," *Journal of Philosophy* 80 (1983) 583-589

Rorty, Richard, "A Reply to Dreyfus and Taylor," *Review of Metaphysics* 34 (1980) 39-46

Rousseau, Jean-Jacques, *Emile* (1762) (London: Dent 1972)

Rousseau, Jean-Jacques, *The First and Second Discourses* (1750 and 1755) (New York: St. Martin's Press 1964)

Rushton, J. Philippe, "Altruism and Society: A Social Learning Perspective," *Ethics* 92 (1982) 459-467)

Bibliography

Rushton, J. Philippe, *Altruism, Socialization, and Society* (Englewood Cliffs, NJ: Prentice-Hall 1980)

Sandel, Michael, *Liberalism and the Limits of Justice* (Cambridge: Cambridge University Press 1982)

Scheler, Max, *Formalism in Ethics and Non-Formal Ethics of Values* (Evanston: Northwestern University Press 1973)

Scherer, K.R., and P. Ekman, *Approaches to Emotion* (Hillsdale, NJ: Lawrence Erlbaum Associates 1984)

Scruton, Roger, *The Meaning of Conservatism* (Harmondsworth, Middlesex: Penguin Books 1980)

Shaffer, Jerome A., "An Assessment of Emotion," *American Philosophical Quarterly* 20 (1983) 161-173

Simpson, Elizabeth Leonie, "Moral Development Research: A Case of Scientific Cultural Bias, *Human Development* 17 (1974) 81-106

Simpson, Evan, ed., *Anti-foundationalism and Practical Reasoning: Conversations Between Hermeneutics and Analysis* (Edmonton: Academic Printing and Publishing 1987)

Simpson, Evan, "The Development of Political Reasoning," *Human Development* 30 (1987) 268-281

Simpson, Evan, "Emile's Moral Development: A Rousseauan Perspective on Kohlberg," *Human Development* 26 (1983) 198-212

Simpson, Evan, "Moral Conservatism," *The Review of Politics* 49 (1987) 29-58

Simpson, Evan, *Reason over Passion: The Social Basis of Evaluation and Appraisal* (Waterloo, Ont.: Wilfrid Laurier University Press 1979)

Simpson, Evan, "The Subjects of Justice," *Ethics* 90 (1980) 590-501

Simpson, Evan, "A Values-Clarification Retrospective," *Educational Theory* 36 (1986) 271-287

Simon, Sidney B., Leland W. Howe, and Howard Kirschenbaum, eds., *Values Clarification: A Handbook of Practical Strategies for Teachers and Students* (New York: Hart Publishing Company 1972)

Smith, Adam, *Theory of Moral Sentiments* (1759) (Oxford: Clarendon Press 1976)

Solomon, Robert C., *The Passions* (Garden City, NY: Anchor Press/Doubleday 1976)

Sommers, Christina Hoff, "Filial Morality," *Journal of Philosophy* 83 (1986) 439-456

Spinoza, Benedict, *Ethics* (1677) (London: Dent 1959)

Stout, Jeffrey, *Ethics After Babel: The Languages of Morals and Their Discontents* (Boston: Beacon Press 1988)

Stout, Jeffrey, "Virtue Among the Ruins," *Neue Zeitschrift für Systematische Theologie* 26 (1984) 256-273

Strauss, Leo, *Natural Right and History* (Chicago: University of Chicago Press 1953)

Sullivan, Edmund V., *Kohlberg's Structuralism: A Critical Appraisal* (Toronto: Ontario Institute for Studies in Education 1977)

Szasz, Thomas, *Ideology and Insanity: Essays on the Psychiatric Dehumanization of Man* (Garden City, NY: Anchor Books 1970)

Tawney, R. H., *Commonplace Book* (Cambridge: Cambridge University Press 1972)

Bibliography

Taylor, Charles, "Explaining Behavior," *Inquiry* 13 (1970) 54-89

Taylor, Charles, *Philosophy and the Human Sciences* (Cambridge: Cambridge University Press 1985)

Taylor, Charles, "Understanding in Human Science," *Review of Metaphysics* 34 (1980) 25-38

Thompson, John B., and David Held, eds., *Habermas: Critical Debates* (London: Macmillan 1982)

Toulmin, Stephen, "The Tyranny of Principles," *The Hastings Center Report* 11, No. 6 (December 1981) 31-39

Tucker, Robert C., ed., *The Marx-Engels Reader* (New York: W.W. Norton, 2nd ed. 1978)

Unger, Roberto Mangabeira, *Knowledge and Politics* (New York: Free Press 1975)

Vygotsky, L.S., *Mind in Society: The Development of Higher Psychological Processes* (Cambridge, MA: Harvard University Press 1978)

Wallace, James D., *Virtues and Vices* (Ithaca: Cornell University Press 1978)

Walzer, Michael, *Spheres of Justice: A Defense of Pluralism and Equality* (New York: Basic Books 1983)

Wiggins, David, "Truth, Invention, and the Meaning of Life," *Proceedings of the British Academy* 62 (1976) 331-378

Williams, Bernard, *Ethics and the Limits of Philosophy* (Cambridge, MA: Harvard University Press 1985)

Williams, Norman, and Sheila Williams, *The Moral Development of Children* (London: Macmillan 1970)

Wittgenstein, Ludwig, *On Certainty* (Oxford: Blackwell 1969)

Wolins, M., and M. Gottesman, eds., *Group Care, An Israeli Approach: The Educational Path of the Youth Aliyah* (New York: Gordon and Breach 1971)

Woodcock, George, *The Crystal Palace: A Study of George Orwell* (Boston: Little, Brown and Co. 1966)

Yeats, W.B., *Collected Poems* (New York: Macmillan 1956)

Youniss, James, "Dialectical Theory and Piaget on Social Knowledge," *Human Development* 21 (1978) 234-247

Index

STUDIES IN MORAL PHILOSOPHY is a book series publishing original works devoted primarily to the problematic or historical examination of the nature of good lives, character and its development, and virtues and vices. The consideration of these and related topics in the light of literary works is particularly welcome. Books in the series are intended to be readily accessible to nonspecialists, and thus they are written in plain English. The editor is:

Professor John Kekes
Department of Philosophy
State University of New York at Albany
Albany, New York 12222

Paul Allen III

PROOF OF MORAL OBLIGATION IN TWENTIETH-CENTURY PHILOSOPHY

American University Studies: Series V (Philosophy). Vol. 45
ISBN 0-8204-0568-X   199 pages   hardback US $ 31.65

Recommended price – alterations reserved

Since Plato's time, philosophers have concentrated on developing moral theories to guide our actions. They have said we ought to act to maximize happiness; we ought to act to fulfill human potential; etc. But all of them have largely ignored a key question: Regardless of *which* acts are morally obligatory, *can moral obligation as such be proven?*

Early in his book, Allen clarifies what sort of demonstration or justification can suffice as a proof that we are subject to moral obligation. He analyzes some twentieth-century ethical theories which initially appear to serve as such a demonstration. Next, he examines at length the theory of contemporary English philosopher R. M. Hare. And finally, he reworks Hare's ideas into a complete proof that we are bound by moral obligation.

Philosophers should value this book because it brings to light and defines a neglected but critical problem, and develops an innovative, thought-provoking solution. Serious students, too, will find it helpful because it provides a clearly written historical study of a central theme in twentieth-century ethics.

PETER LANG PUBLISHING, INC.
62 West 45th Street
USA – New York, NY 10036

William Kluback

DISCOURSES ON THE MEANING OF HISTORY

American University Studies: Series V (Philosophy). Vol. 23

ISBN 0-8204-0387-3   266 pages   hardback US $ 39.00

Recommended price – alterations reserved

Philosophical and Theological essays explore the meaning of history. The author believes that both Philosophy and Theology offer ways to understand the meaning of history. History is our most important intellectual and moral problem. From where we begin to comprehend the significance for man reveals our capacity to understand history.

PETER LANG PUBLISHING, INC.
62 West 45th Street
USA – New York, NY 10036

Walter LaCentra

THE AUTHENTIC SELF
Toward a Philosophy of Personality

American University Studies: Series V (Philosophy). Vol. 36
ISBN 0-8204-0460-8   221 pages   hardback US $ 29.90*

*Recommended price – alterations reserved

This study contends that an adequate theory of personal growth should be based upon a human striving for authenticity, a striving revealed as a dynamic process of self-transcendence operating on three different levels: intellectual, moral, and religious. Just as the act of questioning propels man toward ever newer horizons of wisdom, so also does human and divine love explain the fullness of authentic moral and religious development. Bernard Lonergan's insights into personal development are used to critically evaluate specific aspects of the psychologies of personality developed by Freud, Adler, and Maslow.

Contents: This thesis argues that Lonergan's theory of self-transcendence complements psychological theories of personality – Accent is on the dynamics of human and divine love in building character.

PETER LANG PUBLISHING, INC.
62 West 45th Street
USA — New York, NY 10036